P9-EMP-009

ALSO FROM
THE NAPOLEON HILL FOUNDATION
AND BALLANTINE BOOKS

Think & Grow Rich
by Napoleon Hill

Think and Grow Rich: A Black Choice
by Dennis Kimbro and Napoleon Hill

THINK
& GROW
RICH
A Latino Choice

THINK
& GROW
RICH

A Latino Choice

Lionel Sosa,
with The Napoleon Hill Foundation

BALLANTINE BOOKS

New York

A Ballantine Books Trade Paperback Original

Copyright © 2006 by The Napoleon Hill Foundation

All rights reserved.

Published in the United States by Ballantine Books, an imprint of The Random House Publishing Group, a division of Random House, Inc., New York.

BALLANTINE and colophon are registered trademarks of Random House, Inc.

Library of Congress Cataloging-in-Publication Data
Sosa, Lionel.
    Think and grow rich : a Latino choice / Lionel Sosa ; with The Napoleon Hill Foundation.
        p. cm.
    "A Ballantine Books trade pbk. original"—T.p. verso.
    ISBN 0-345-48561-0
    1. Hispanic Americans—Economic conditions.   2. Hispanic Americans—Life skills guides.   3. Success.   4. Hill, Napoleon, 1883–1970—Philosophy. 5. Hill, Napoleon, 1883–1970—Influence.   I. Napoleon Hill Foundation. II. Title.
    E184.S75S67 2006
    650.1'208968073—dc22   2005055879

Printed in the United States of America

www.ballantinebooks.com

9 8 7 6 5 4 3 2 1

Text design by Mauna Eichner

To the love of my life,
my dear wife,
Kathy Sosa,
who looked over every page
of this book and helped
make it infinitely better.

Foreword

As executive director of the Napoleon Hill Foundation, I decided to publish a book targeted to the growing Hispanic population of the world. I had subscribed to a Hispanic magazine and had been reading books by Hispanic authors. I wanted the book to be based on the success principles that Dr. Napoleon Hill had studied, applied, and introduced in one of his most famous books, *Think & Grow Rich*. Written in 1937, it has sold in excess of twenty-five million copies and remains a bestseller today.

I mentioned my desire to find a Hispanic author familiar with Dr. Hill's work to Phil Fuentes, a trustee of the Napoleon Hill Foundation. He arranged for me to meet with Lionel Sosa, author of *The Americano Dream: How Latinos Can Achieve Success in Business and in Life*. After I had met and talked with Lionel in Chicago, it was obvious to me that he was the right person to write a success book for and about the dynamic Hispanic population.

Lionel had become familiar with Napoleon Hill's writings when he was painting for a sign company and making $1.10 per hour. He used the Hill philosophy of success to form his own business, which grew to be the largest Hispanic advertising company in the United States.

When you read about Lionel Sosa and understand his accomplishments, you should recall the statement from Napoleon Hill: "There is nothing that belief, plus a burning desire, cannot make real."

Lionel's story, and those of other outstanding Hispanics, will illustrate how you too can discover that where you have been is not as important as where you are going. Sosa will show you how to travel in the right direction.

As you read these stories, study the principles of success that their subjects used to reach their goals. Reading about the accomplishments of others will inspire you to realize that if you study and apply the principles, you too can attain success. Each successful person has had to overcome adversity to reach success. Your journey will most likely be no different.

The best to you. Always believe that while living in one of the greatest countries in the world, following the principles Sosa so intelligently writes about will only make your journey easier and more enjoyable.

DON M. GREEN
Executive Director
Napoleon Hill Foundation

Contents

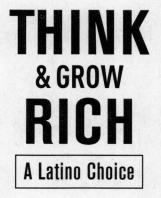

THINK
& GROW
RICH

A Latino Choice

The Five Minutes
That Changed My Life

The first time I heard about *Think & Grow Rich,* I was twenty-three years old. Married with two kids and another on the way, I was doing what I thought I should be doing—working like hell to earn a living. The year was 1963 and minimum wage was a dollar an hour. I was doing better than that: $1.10. I was okay with that. I had a desk job as a neon sign designer at a small shop called Texas Neon. Still, my weekly take-home pay after taxes and deductions was only $37.50, hardly enough to make ends meet. I worried every day and prayed, hoping one of the kids wouldn't get sick. How would I pay the doctor?

One day, I got lucky. A woman by the name of Sally Pond came into the shop and asked us to design a small sign for her office building. She wanted it to read, "The School of Personal Achievement." As she explained her business, my ears perked up. She promised that anyone who took the course and followed the teachings of Napoleon Hill and his seventeen principles of personal achievement would get rich. Every bit as rich as he or she wanted.

Napoleon Hill? Who was that? Was he French? Was he related to Bonaparte? Was he dead?

"No," she said. "This man is alive, living in Chicago. And as far as I'm concerned, he's more important than Napoleon Bonaparte. *This Napoleon will make you a millionaire.*"

In about five minutes, Sally Pond signed me up. And in those five minutes, my life changed. Not only did I get a chance to design her sign, I got a chance to design my life, and to acquire the knowledge I would need to lead a happy life and earn millions. I borrowed the money to pay for the course, joining fifteen other would-be millionaires at the Napoleon Hill School of Personal Achievement. Those seventeen weeks in class changed my life forever.

Hill's mantra was: "Whatever your mind can conceive and believe, you can achieve." I believed every word. After all, his philosophy was not just one man's opinion. It was the shared wisdom distilled from the minds of hundreds of the most successful people in the world. Napoleon Hill had spent more than twenty years compiling this treasure. He had spent hours, days, and weeks interviewing presidents, heads of state, inventors, and captains of industry. His work was a gold mine of information and success secrets.

My eyes were as wide as baseballs. The excitement inside me was huge. Imagine. I could be rich! I could be happy! I could make important contributions to society by learning and applying Hill's seventeen principles of personal achievement! Even before the first day of class, something inside me began to change. For the first time in my life, instead of worrying, I was thinking positively about the future.

The course was taught in seventeen installments. Every Monday, we would report promptly at 5 p.m., and each week we were introduced to a new lesson. With each lesson, we learned a new principle. During the first twenty minutes of instruction, we were shown a 16-mm movie of Mr. Hill giving an overview of the lesson of the week. Week one: Definiteness of Purpose. Week two: The Mastermind Alliance. And so on. Class discussion was encouraged, and the conversations were spirited. We had workbooks to fill out and homework to do. Sally invited successful people to guest lecture and tell their stories of how their dreams had come true by applying Hill's principles. Many of the students became good friends, though we didn't socialize much after class. We tended to rush home to do our homework and get ready for the following week.

Had I been older and more experienced, I might have been skeptical of the whole philosophy. I might have questioned some of it as being too simple, such as the idea that *you can achieve whatever your mind believes you can achieve.* I might have questioned some of the instruction as being too offbeat, such as the concept of autosuggestion, the idea that *you can talk yourself into believing anything, good or bad.* Being young and naïve can be a great asset. For me, it was a blessing. I didn't question anything. My mind was open. I drank it all in.

Whatever your age, experience, or level of maturity, pretend you're a kid again as you read this book. Keep an open mind. Don't come on this journey carrying the baggage of cynicism and doubt. Understand that baggage of this sort is the by-product of experience and rationalism—behaviors we learn as adults. This baggage is too heavy to take on our trip to success and riches. Lose it.

Also, soak up all seventeen principles. You may not master them all. That's okay. Several of the people I interviewed for this book (many of whom are disciples of Napoleon Hill and *Think & Grow Rich*) tell me that they apply no more than a handful of these principles each day. But they do apply them each day. That's what's important. Looking back, I realize that I have mastered only four of them. Yet, those four were so powerful, they were all that I needed and exactly what I needed. Later in the book, I'll tell you which four I mastered and how they continue to work for me.

Latinos and Success

Perhaps you're reading this book because you are Latino or Hispanic. Perhaps you are simply curious about the almost fifty million of us who reside in the United States and Puerto Rico. Maybe you want insights into the one billion of us who inhabit the continents known as the Americas. Did you know that the Americas are two-thirds Latino?

Note that I use Latino and Hispanic interchangeably. Personally, I prefer "Latino." I agree with the comedian George Lopez, who shies away from the term "Hispanic" because it has the word *panic* in it.

Why do Latinos need their own version of *Think & Grow Rich,* a book that has been around since the 1930s and has helped turn tens of thousands of ordinary people into leaders and millionaires? Italians didn't get their own version. Jews didn't. Why Latinos?

Good question. Two reasons:

1. No group of people is *better prepared* to take advantage of *Think & Grow Rich* than Latinos.
2. On the other hand, no group of people is *more poorly prepared* to take advantage of *Think & Grow Rich* than Latinos.

Sound crazy? It's really not. Let me explain.

Latinos in the United States have a lot to be proud of. We are the largest minority population in the nation. That makes us big and powerful. We've come a long way since the days when restaurants would hang signs that read, "No Mexicans or Dogs Allowed."

Today, there's plenty of good news: Hispanic income is at an all-time high. So is our buying power, and also our home-ownership levels. Our entrepreneurial spirit is legend. Every year, Latinos start more small businesses than any other group of Americans. We have the political power that has helped elect two presidents. Latinos are big in popular culture, music, entertainment, and the arts. Many Anglos aspire to be Latino. It's wonderful!

Some of the news is not, however. Our high school- and college-completion rates are the lowest of any ethnic group. We earn less money per capita than non-Latinos. Few of us are represented on corporate boards or in top management. Our immigration woes still get national attention.

Professor Samuel P. Huntington of Harvard University wrote a book titled *Who Are We?* In it, he depicts Latinos as a menace to all that America has achieved and represents. He disagrees with my position that the Americano Dream is for everyone to share and says so in his book. "[Sosa] is wrong," he says. "There is no Americano Dream. There is only an American Dream created by an Anglo-Protestant society. Mexican Americans will share in that dream and in that society only if they dream in English."

Who says Mexican Americans don't dream in English? We dream in two languages, and English is one of them. It is Dr. Huntington who is wrong. Dead wrong. Latinos are attracted to America for the same reason every other immigrant has ever been: for the opportunity to make it big, based on our own talent, heart, hard work, and initiative.

For all the press we get, good and bad, very little is known about who we really are. Truth is, we know precious little about ourselves. How many of us know that Hispanics settled in North

America seventy-eight years before the Pilgrims ever landed at Plymouth Rock? Or that Spain and its territories such as Mexico and Cuba, in large part, financed the American Revolution? Or that Puerto Ricans, Mexicans, Cubans, and other Latinos together have earned more congressional medals of honor to date defending our country? How many Americans can name a dozen of the fifteen hundred cities and four states in the United States with Spanish names? We know the city of San Franciso by its Spanish name. Otherwise, we'd call it St. Francis. The same is true for the state of Nevada. In English, it would be called Snowfall. Hispanics named those cities and states because we were in North America before the British. Spanish-speaking Americans comprise the third-largest Spanish-speaking "country," right behind Mexico and Spain.

That's just the beginning. What's more important is who we are now, how we think, and how our success will impact this America.

The Latino Experience

Let's get down to business. Just who are Latinos? For starters, we are a complicated group—an amalgamation of people from twenty-five countries throughout Mexico, South and Central America, and the Caribbean, as well as Spain, and Portugal. As we grow and become part of the mainstream, we become more complicated, more difficult to understand.

Some gringos (I use the term affectionately) think we are aliens. To many Latin Americans, we are some sort of gringo hybrid who has forsaken the mother country. Other minorities in the United States are easier to understand, perhaps because they share a common experience, and often a common injury. For Jewish Americans, it is the Holocaust. African Americans get their sense of identity and unity from slavery. Even non-minorities have their symbols: Texans have the Alamo, Southerners have Appomattox.

What do Latinos have? As Cantinflas, the Mexican comedian, used to say, *"Allí está el detalle."* Loosely translated, this is a hedge that really means "who knows?" Our story is hard to define. Our injury is not apparent. Yet it must be there. Why else would we be labeled a minority even in cities like San Antonio where we have always been a majority? Why else would we have higher levels of poverty and lower levels of achievement?

The experts all have answers. Some say the situation is caused by the steady wave of new immigrants who enter this country poor and undereducated. Others say Latinos are inhibited by lower expectations of themselves and of their children that stem from their history and culture. Still others dismiss us as simple optimists who measure success differently. Roberto Suro, in his book *Strangers Among Us,* believes that whereas we may see ourselves as being respectful, American society sees us as being subservient. Raul Yzaguirre, founder of the National Council of La Raza, believes that the "system" works against Latinos and that prejudice and lack of adequate government funding is to blame.

Maybe they are all right. But there's something else that impacts our low economic status. My own research of the last twenty years indicates it may have to do with a lack of self-identity. And thus a lack of self-confidence. Did the conquest of the Indian by the Spaniards and Portuguese leave an imprint that makes us feel less worthy today? To explore this issue, we must peel back the onion. One layer at a time. Even if it hurts.

Noted theologian Father Virgilio Elizondo often makes this observation in his writings:

> We are the *mestizaje* or "mixture" of the Spanish and the indigenous native of the Americas. As such, we were both the welcomers and the welcomed. We were both the explored and the explorers. We were both the settlers and the settled. We were both the conquered

and the conquerors. We were both the victims and the victimizers. We are the mother and the father as well as the children of this land we call the USA.

And because our origin is so new—500 years, compared to Europe's 48,000 years—*we were here to witness and record our own conception, as well as our own birth.*

Pretty heady stuff, huh? Father Virgil is a genius (you'll find his story in the final chapter of this book). Examining his insights, two big things jump out at me:

1. *We share a uniquely Latino injury, the conquest.* It produced an unconscious macho/servant dichotomy. We can be as tough as a conqueror one minute and meek as a slave the next. In public, many of us put on our subservient hats. At home, the macho steel helmet.
2. *We share a uniquely Latino characteristic.* Our quiet but relentless energy and optimism arose from the need to survive in the face of recurring oppression.

Now let's see how we can make these observations work for us in terms of thinking and growing rich.

Making *Think & Grow Rich* Work for You

The cultural baggage derived from our roots subtly influences our successes and failures. Our roots make us who we are. They determine our core values. These values dictate our beliefs, and our beliefs drive our behavior.

Are you carrying negative cultural baggage on your journey to riches? Are you carrying some you are unaware of?

To make *Think & Grow Rich* work for you as a Latino, first understand what makes us tick:

1. our unconscious servant/macho psyche
2. our relentless energy and optimism
3. our values compared to Anglo values

Let's explore these points, one at a time.

1. Our Unconscious Servant/Macho Psyche

Many Latinos get upset when I bring up the concept of "unconscious servitude" (although they don't seem to mind the "macho" part as much). They assume I'm putting down our value system. Nothing could be further from the truth. I love our conservative core values. I believe them. I embrace them. But I always press on.

"Okay, tell me something. What did your parents teach you to say when an adult called your name?"

> *"Mande usted."*
> "What does *'mande usted'* mean?" I ask.
> "It means, 'Yes?' It's an acknowledgment."
> "Come on, what does it really mean? Think!"
> "It means, 'Huh?' Only much more respectful."
> "Think," I urge.
> I spell it out. *M-A-N-D-E—M-E.*
> "Command me? Order me?"
> Oops!

Have you ever heard an Anglo parent calling out to a child and the child responding, "Order me?" Of course not. Yet we Latinos say it every day. Gladly. Thinking we're being respectful. Kids respond to their elders that way. Workers to their bosses. Maids to the ladies of the house. It's so engrained, that even after we realize what we're saying, many of us keep right on saying it.

Other examples of this phenomenon:

> *A sus órdenes,* "At your command."
> *Para servirle,* "Here to serve you."
> *Con su permiso,* "With your permission."
> *Como usted mande,* "As you command."
> *Por nada,* "For nothing," after *Gracias* or "Thank you."

In Mexico, we're being respectful. In the United States, we're being subservient. That's unconscious servitude! There's no disgrace in being polite and service-oriented. In fact, it's good for business. However, as Latinos, we must be very aware of the fine line between being service conscious and having a subservient consciousness.

Note that the *Mande usted* phenomenon applies to Mexico, Central America, and the northern cone of South America—that is, where the mixing of the races occurred after the conquest. It is not a term used in all of Latin America.

2. Our Relentless Energy and Optimism

In most of Latin America, the average Joe *(José)* and *Josefina* get their feet cut out from under them every time they're about to get ahead of the game. Frequent and major monetary devaluations are common. From one day to the next, their money can become virtually worthless. Devaluations usually happen when governments are being handed over from one administration to the next. People lose their savings, their homes, and their futures.

What do they do? They start over. *Tenemos que seguir adelante,*

"We must continue forward," they sigh. And they do move forward. Their faith in God and love of family keeps their hopes alive.

That's relentless energy and optimism! It's in every one of us. And we can make it pay off when we understand the principles of *Think & Grow Rich*.

3. Our Values Compared to Anglo American Values

It's important that we are aware of these values, where they diverge, where they converge, and the roots that drive them. Latino values are based on Catholicism, Spanish colonialism, and respect for authority. It is a culture of interdependence and of personal responsibility that focuses on family closeness.

- family first
- family helps family
- total faith in God
- humility
- work hard
- sacrifice
- stability
- respect for authority
- modesty
- God loves the poor
- I accept life's problems
- small success is good
- whatever God wants
- I hope someday . . .

The Anglo American culture is quite different. It is based on the formation of a new free and independent nation where "all men are created equal." Individuality and freedom of expression are huge. Anglo American values are rooted in Puritan, Protestant, and Calvinistic philosophies that promote the idea that those who are born rich, or have made themselves rich, are especially blessed. And because they are blessed, they have a responsibility to the greater society.

- individualism
- helping self helps family
- faith in self *and* in God
- self-expression
- working smart
- paying your dues
- What's new? What's next?
- challenge authority
- toot your own horn
- God loves the rich, too
- I solve life's problems
- big success is better
- what I want
- I will achieve

These core values are almost taken for granted country by country. And while they are not written in stone anywhere, they quietly and deeply influence the beliefs and behavior of the citizenry.

When you put the Latino values and the Anglo American values side by side, an amazing thing happens. A tension is created by the bipolar natures of the two sets of value systems. The following chart illustrates this.

Latino Values	Anglo Values
Based on Catholicism, Spanish colonialism, and respect for tradition	Based on Puritan, Protestant, and Calvinistic thinking of a new and free America
INTERDEPENDENCE	INDEPENDENCE

Family First	Me First
Family Helps Family	Helping Self Helps Family
Faith in God	Faith in Self and in God
Humility	Self-Expression
Work Hard	Work Smart
Sacrifice	Pay Your Dues
Stability	What's New? What's Next?
Respect for Authority	Challenge Authority
Modesty	Toot Your Horn
God Loves the Poor	God Loves the Rich, Too
I Accept Life's Problems	I Solve Life's Problems
Small Success is Good	Big Success is Better
Whatever God Wants	What I Want, Too!
I Hope to Achieve	I Believe I Will Achieve
Vergüenza	What's that?
Sacrificio	To a Point
Sufrimiento	Avoid At All Costs
Sudor	Okay, But Not Forever
Responsabilidad	Of Course
Respeto	Earn it First

"Lo Que Dios Quiera"	"The Sky Is the Limit"

Look at the bottom section of the chart. The words on the left in Spanish are very familiar to Latinos. They are: Shame, Sacrifice,

Suffering, Sweat. These words are baggage. We use them often—
especially *vergüenza,* which means shame. We use it so often, in
fact, that we don't hear it—only a person learning Spanish can pick
it up, particularly if they're overhearing a conversation.

My wife Kathy has a little story about that. She is an Anglo girl
from Alabama and came to San Antonio when she was fifteen.
She'd never seen a Mexican before. She became fascinated with the
accent and dark skin and hung around Mexican families a lot.
When she visited a friend's home, the family's conversation turned
to Spanish. Kathy was trying to understand what they were saying
and asked her friend, "What is this word? Everybody keeps saying
it—*Qué vergüenza! No tiene vergüenza! Sin vergüenza!*"

I almost fell over when Kathy first told me this story. "Oh, my
God, shame is a bigger part of our lives than I thought!"

Could it be that a needless feeling of shame was drummed into
the heads of our ancestors by their conquerors five hundred years
ago? Could it be that even the Aztecs, Incas, and Mayans inculcated
the feeling in the minds of their slaves to keep them subservient?
Sounds plausible. The amazing thing is that these thoughts and
feelings are still with us five hundred years later. We were taught a
new language. A new religion. And a new way to act. *Mande usted.*

Now you know all the baggage.

Lose it for good.

You are ready to think and grow rich!

Definiteness of Purpose
—Charles Patrick Garcia

If you have read the foreword, you know this book is based on the work of my hero, Napoleon Hill, who spent his entire life learning the ways of some of the world's most successful people. He then took the wisdom he collected and distilled it into seventeen clearly defined principles for success. His findings have proven to be so accurate and practical that today *Think & Grow Rich* and *Napoleon Hill's Law to Success* continue to be among the world's bestselling motivational books.

Why? Because they are as relevant today as they were the day he introduced them. Tens of thousands of people have adapted these principles, put them to work, and achieved success beyond their dreams. If you want to achieve success, this book will show you how.

Once Napoleon Hill identified the seventeen principles of personal achievement, he put them in order of importance. Heading the list was "definiteness of purpose," and for good reason. After years of interviewing the super-successful, he discovered that they all built their fortunes based on this common characteristic: *They had a definite purpose.*

The Advantages of Definiteness of Purpose

All seventeen principles are important, to be sure. But make no mistake, you won't get to first base without having a definite major purpose. A definite purpose is more than a strong wish. It is *a clear, definite goal fueled by great passion.* Definiteness of purpose focuses all your energy on making your goal your reality. It makes you believe. When you believe, you forget your doubts and fears. Pessimistic thoughts vanish and optimistic thoughts become habit.

Lo que Dios quiera is not a definite purpose. Neither is *Como lo quiera Dios.* "I want to be happy" is not a definite purpose. Those are wishes. Do not confuse wishes with real purpose and real goals. That would be like trying to build a cathedral with only a sketch on a napkin as your guide. Your contractors would make so many mistakes and adjustments trying to interpret your sketch that you could never be sure of the result. Your cathedral might get built, but probably not the way you wanted it.

How to Find Your Purpose

How do you find your definite purpose? Is it difficult? Does it come easy? How do you know when you have found it? Let's look at a Hispanic success story that inspires and motivates.

Charles Patrick Garcia is the author of the *Wall Street Journal* bestselling book, *A Message From Garcia: Yes, You Can Succeed.* If you have never heard of this man, keep your ears and eyes open.

In the mid-1990s, he founded a financial services company in an empty broom closet. Number of employees: three. As I write this chapter in the summer of 2004, his Florida-based Sterling Financial Investment Group has sixty offices in seven countries and some four hundred employees. His company, with a large Latino customer base, provides research, trading counseling, investment banking, and wealth management.

The journey that brought him to this lofty destination was full of unexpected twists and turns. Garcia was born and raised in Panama. He came to the United States in 1979 to enroll in the U.S. Air Force Academy. He served as a highly decorated military officer in Central America in the 1980s. He earned a master's degree in public administration. He was a White House Fellow and attended Columbia law school. All while in his twenties.

Here's where his story takes an unusual turn. In 1994, having just graduated from law school, he had a promising future. He had been offered a clerkship for a federal judge in Florida. His bags were packed. He was ready to move with his wife and two-month-old daughter from New York to Miami. At midnight Charles Garcia changed his mind.

Don't misunderstand. He knew he could be a good lawyer. Even a great one. His success in law school had proven that. But something didn't sit right. He just wasn't feeling passionate about a career in law.

Listen to Your Gut and Be Alert to Opportunity

Charles began listening to his gut. He knew he wanted something else, but didn't yet know exactly what. Maybe that's what you're feeling as you read this book. If so, do what Charles did. He took an aptitude test. One called the Myers-Briggs Personality Type Indicator test. It showed a natural bent for leadership and entrepreneurial pursuits, not law. This idea excited him. It stirred passion and desire in his heart. *Ganas,* as the great educator Jaime Escalante prefers to call it.

"I could have been a good lawyer," Garcia explains, "but 'good' wasn't good enough. To truly succeed you must follow your heart.

You can earn a living, even a good one, doing what's expected. But you can't gain great wealth without having a deep, burning passion. Without true definiteness of purpose."

The choice became clear. His own passion would drive him, not the expectations of others. So Garcia went into business instead of law. When he shared his decision with his family, his father-in-law Seymour Holtzman made a suggestion—that Garcia apprentice with him for a few years to gain some hands-on experience. Holtzman was a brilliant, self-made businessman who had built and operated a number of successful companies. Garcia knew he must seize this opportunity. Holtzman became his mentor.

Get Good Advice, Find Good Mentors

"My father was the first to introduce me to the concept of mentoring," Garcia writes in his book. Charles's father's mentor had been Dr. Charles Huffnagel, a top heart surgeon who treated presidents Eisenhower and Kennedy. "Mentoring is a good way to find out if a career is as glamorous up close as it is from afar was the lesson learned." Charles continues, "Mentoring gives you a firsthand look into the field that excites you. It helps you see the good, the bad, and the ugly up close. It helps you separate the dream from the reality. It gives you a chance to evaluate your choice."

Aside from his father-in-law, another of Charles's mentors was General John Galvin, a four-star general who later became NATO supreme allied commander. "One of the biggest lessons I learned from General Galvin was to always think of at least three solutions for every problem, and then choose one over the other two," remarks Garcia. "That way, you can be sure you're not grasping at the first solution that comes to mind."

You can use that bit of advice in choosing your definite purpose. Don't pick the first idea that pops into your head that seems exciting. Think of at least another two paths you can take and be passionate about. Evaluate the plusses and minuses of each one. Only then should you choose one over the other.

Another of Charles Garcia's mentors was John C. Whitehead, former Goldman Sachs CEO. Garcia worked for him while serving as a White House Fellow. Whitehead influenced his decision to go into financial services, and when Garcia founded Sterling Financial in 1997, he put into practice what he learned from Whitehead. Something called the "culture of success," a set of philosophical principles that had taken Goldman Sachs to the top of the Wall Street ladder.

William Bennett, President George H. W. Bush's "Drug Czar" and bestselling author, was still another mentor.

"From Bill Bennett I learned the value of getting out from behind the desk and getting my hands dirty," says Garcia. "I learned the importance of setting high goals without fear of the repercussions. I even learned the importance of balancing work with play. My colleagues and I played many spirited games of touch football with him."

So what does all this mean to you? In deciding on your definite purpose, take the time to seek out a mentor. Or two or three. Work as closely as you can with him or her. Don't wait for someone to come to you. Go out and find one. You'll be amazed at how willing they can be to help you define your definite purpose.

The Power of the Subconscious

Garcia believes that reading stories about people who believed and achieved can provide a life-altering dose of inspiration. Indeed, his book, *A Message From Garcia,* includes a tapestry of such anecdotes that illustrates his success beliefs and success principles.

"When you read about men and women who succeeded against all odds, or who made amazing strides and advances, it gives you hope," he says. "You think, 'If he can do it, or if she can do it, why not me?' And it's true. It's our subconscious mind at work. We all have that incredible inner resource at our disposal. To fail to access it out of laziness or apathy or fear is shameful."

I asked Garcia if he could give me several examples of people whose stories might prove motivational to Latinos.

"I have three examples," Garcia replied. "First, a Latino who has achieved greatness. Second, a successful immigrant. Third, a non-Hispanic with our hopes and dreams with a strategy that any Latino can model."

Putting Definiteness of Purpose to Work

Wenceslao Casares is a shining example of bold thinking and definiteness of purpose. He was born to a family of sheep ranchers in Patagonia, Argentina. At age twenty, he had dropped out of college to pursue his entrepreneurial dream, to found a personal finance website.

He was working as a bellboy in Argentina when he began looking for money to finance his new company. Raising the capital for such a radical and unproven idea like an online brokerage firm was a big challenge in those days. The Internet was in its infancy and nobody could be sure whether the concept would ever be successful.

Tough as it was, he and his partner Constancio Larguia persevered. They never wavered. They never backed down. They never gave up. They believed in their idea with all their might. They stayed the course no matter how bleak things looked. It took the partners a year to raise the one million dollars they needed to get started. They were ready to prove their concept was sound.

Their definiteness of purpose paid off. By early 2000, at the age of twenty-six, Casares and his partner sold 75 percent of the business to Banco Santander of Spain for an estimated $580 million!

Casares had a technique. Beginning at age seventeen, he would sit down every year and ask himself: "If I knew I couldn't fail, what goal would I set?" He would fantasize. Visualize. Dramatize. Anything was possible. Why? Because he did all this with the idea that he couldn't fail!

His next step was to carefully commit his dreams and goals to paper. This made them seem more real than ever. He went a little further, plotting on paper the steps needed to achieve his dream. He reviewed his plan frequently, and each year in January he would repeat the exercise.

One of his early dreams as a young boy was to buy a sailboat and sail around the world. He kept focused on this goal, and on May 18, 2004, he left a marina in Miami, to journey around the world on his forty-four-foot-long catamaran.

Creating a Plan

On the back cover of Garcia's book is an endorsement from Arnold Schwarzenegger. It reads in part: "America is the land of opportunity. I came to this country with empty pockets, a head filled with dreams and a desire to succeed. I tell young people all the time that if you believe in yourself, you can do anything."

If the American Dream is about creating your own destiny, Schwarzenegger is the perfect example. He had a plan. Every amazing goal he has set for himself, he has attained through definiteness of purpose. Born in 1947 in Austria, he got his start as a champion bodybuilder by working out in conditions so cold that his hands froze to the weights. He had a goal: to be the greatest and most famous bodybuilder ever. He won numerous awards and was crowned Mr. Universe a record five times! He promoted his feat with the movie, the cult classic, *Pumping Iron.*

In 1968, Schwarzenegger came to America. He had a new definite purpose: to become a successful businessperson. He accomplished it with lightning speed, quickly establishing himself as a successful real estate entrepreneur. His next two goals were to marry a member of the Kennedy family and to become a movie star.

Outlandish! Impossible! How could he do this? His English skills were sorely lacking. He had no real experience as an actor. His only movie was a documentary, and in it, he had not needed to act. All he had to do was to work out and compete in bodybuilding contests while the camera followed him around. To him, this lack of experience was not a barrier. Why? He believed. He had definiteness of purpose.

Because Arnold first conceived, and only then believed, he achieved the impossible. He got his way. In 1984, he hit the big time with his first *Terminator* film. It was only the first of many blockbuster movies that catapulted him into Hollywood superstardom. Soon after, he married a Kennedy—Maria Shriver—a union that surprised many, considering he is a Republican and she a member of the biggest Democrat dynasty in American history. But perhaps his grandest accomplishment came in 2003, when Schwarzenegger was elected governor of the state of California with a record number of Latino votes. In fact, with more Latino votes than any other Republican in California history.

"Arnold is proof positive that if you can conceive it, you can achieve it," adds Garcia. "He is an inspiration to any first-generation American—really, to anyone. He continues to inspire me."

Success Is a Worthy Goal

Charles D. Kelman, physician, inventor, musician, and entertainer died on June 1, 2004, at age seventy-four. He may seem an unlikely candidate to group with a young dot-com entrepreneur like Casares or a high-profile celebrity-politician like Schwarzenegger, but Garcia says that the late Kelman had a tremendous influence on his own life and career.

"If there is one message I want to get across to anyone, it's that anything you want to achieve is there for the taking," Garcia explains. "The power exists in your subconscious mind. The key is figuring out how to get your conscious mind to believe it and accept it."

Kelman's story begins in his early childhood, when he developed an insatiable craving for the spotlight. Loving the feeling of making people happy, he began performing for his family as a singer, a saxophonist, and a comedian. Kelman's father knew that he had a creative, artistic, and inventive son, but he believed young Charles's talents should be used to serve others. So he told his son that before he became an entertainer or artist, he must first become a doctor.

A product of a time when a child obeyed his father without question, Kelman complied. He ended up studying medicine at the University of Geneva in Switzerland. Yet he never gave up his first dream. While attending medical school, he played saxophone in bars and nightclubs. After he graduated and returned to the United States to become an ophthalmic physician and eye surgeon, he continued to pursue his passion for music.

Ultimately, Kelman created a life that blended both pursuits. He became a pioneer in cataract surgery. He won numerous awards for his medical successes. He gained worldwide fame as an inventor with more than 150 patents to his name. And he also went on to record music professionally, perform at Carnegie Hall, produce Broadway shows, and entertain on top network television shows including *The Tonight Show, The David Letterman Show,* and *Oprah.*

How did Kelman achieve his incredible feats? He learned the importance of writing down your goals and reviewing them several times a day.

One of his ten original goals was international recognition for a major breakthrough in the medical field. Another was to have fun and be successful with music. Others included a happy marriage and children, financial security, and excellent physical health. He achieved them all.

"Would Dr. Kelman have reached his goals without a definiteness of purpose? Without writing them down and reviewing them three to six times a day? Probably not," Garcia concludes. "Clearly articulating his goals allowed him to focus his thoughts and actions on them. Yes, his perseverance played a critical role, but without the act of putting pen to paper he wouldn't have had the clarity needed to push his goals forward."

Creating Opportunity

Garcia's admiration for Charles Kelman amounts to far more than lip service. The "writing it down" technique that brought the physician such rewards has become something of a Garcia trademark. In the speeches he gives to various audiences—whose interests range from education to Latino issues to personal and business success— he emphasizes the importance of writing down and visualizing one's dreams.

In fact, Garcia has developed a web-based software program called Success Compass that stimulates people to dream about everything they would like to accomplish in their lifetime. The program, which is available at www.successisforme.com, is free to anyone wishing to create opportunity by activating his or her subconscious mind to turn dreams into reality. The program sparks your imagination by first asking the simple question: "What would you want to accomplish in your life if you knew you could not fail?" As you continue, the program prompts you to set specific goals in areas such as spiritual well-being, physical health, and finances. Next, you prioritize them until you come up with your top ten. To keep your goals in front of you, Success Compass e-mails them back to you three times a day! I love the way technology can help us be more disciplined.

"Just the act of visiting the website seems to help people articulate and crystallize their goals," Garcia explains. "And when you open your e-mail and you see your goals in front of you, you reflect on them anew, you recommit yourself to them. When you're truly committed, you will make decisions and take actions that lead you to the fulfillment of those dreams. It's a very, very simple principle. Amazingly, it's one that very few people embrace."

And that, my friend, is the biggest tragedy of all. If you settle for the ordinary, that's exactly what you'll get. Most people settle for less than they are capable of accomplishing. That's because they don't take the time to set their goals or to create their definiteness of purpose. They leave their future to destiny. They make excuses. They procrastinate. They don't muster the courage. This isn't a problem that plagues Latinos exclusively. It affects over 95 percent of the human population. I predict you are part of the 5 percent setting high expectations. Not only that, I believe you will achieve those high expectations. Why? Because you are reading this book. This is the first step to success!

Napoleon Hill taught us that our most valuable natural resource is not our natural forests or our mineral deposits. It is the power of our minds. He taught us that if we can conceive and believe, we can achieve. It's true! Charles Garcia knows it. I know it, and so do the many thousands of super-successful people the world over who follow Napoleon Hill's teachings. You can get started today—by determining your definite purpose.

3

The Mastermind Alliance
—Ernest Bromley

When I was twenty-three years old, I believed I could make things happen all by myself. I thought I didn't need help from anybody. Perhaps I had taken my mother's advice too literally. She always said, "Lionel, whatever you want to do, you will be able to do." I must have heard it a million times.

To me, the message was clear: "Whatever *you* want to do." Not "whatever *you and several other people* want to do." My father's influence emphasized the point. He ran his dry cleaning shop pretty much single-handedly. He worked twelve-hour days, six days a week, and took no vacations. When he needed help, he hired free-lance people.

Up to that point, I'd been doing okay following Mom's advice and Dad's example. In school, my grades had been good. Sometimes straight As. I'd graduated from high school as a lieutenant colonel in the ROTC as well as the foreman of my commercial art class. At my first job, I had already gotten a raise and won praise for my work. And I had done it all myself. The thought of needing others to help me succeed had not entered my mind.

This was all about to change.

The mastermind alliance first came on to my radar screen when I signed up for Napoleon Hill's course, The Science of Personal Achievement, taught in San Antonio by Sally Pond. There I saw and heard Hill describe this important principle on film: "The mastermind alliance is built of two or more minds working together in *perfect harmony* in pursuit of a common goal. This concept allows you to use the talents, experience, knowledge, and education of the people you work with to help you reach your goal. The combined energy turns beliefs into reality."

After class, I took Sally aside. "What is he talking about? This doesn't apply to me. I can achieve my goals myself. Always have." Sally Pond spoke gently. "Step back and listen," she said. "Open your mind. You're in this course to learn, right?"

"Okay, I'll try."

I began to block out my old beliefs as best I could in order to soak up this new thinking. It wasn't easy. When I finally understood it, it became clear. I began to reconstruct the important events in my life. Soon I realized my error. I had not been doing well in school and at work all by myself! I just thought I had. My parents, teachers, schoolmates, family, and coworkers had been encouraging me and mentoring me all along. I just never stopped long enough to realize it. Without them, there would have been no As. No real success in school or at my job.

My mind opened up. I accepted the truth and became a believer. As you read this book, I urge you to do the same. Become a believer. When you do, magic happens all around you. New doors of opportunity open at every turn. You don't have to read your horoscope or open fortune cookies to find your future full of success, happiness, and fulfillment. You'll be literally writing your own fortune.

There isn't a person living or dead who has achieved great success by himself. Every Latino highlighted in this book will tell you the same thing.

The world-renowned author Sandra Cisneros didn't become a great writer all by herself, even though she writes the books. She needs her literary agent, her publisher, her editor, and the inspiration she gets from her many readers. She needs the memories of her experiences to encourage her and her pets to comfort her.

Moctesuma Esparza, the producer of great movies like *The Milagro Beanfield War, Selena, Gettysburg,* and *Gods and Generals* among many others, cannot bring a movie to the screen on his own. He needs financiers, great actors, directors, crew members, distributors, and theaters.

Bill Richardson, the Latino governor of New Mexico and former U.S. representative to the United Nations, could not have won his gubernatorial race without a great staff, supportive family, volunteers, and—of course—the voters.

Like them, you will need to form a mastermind alliance to find real success. You will not succeed by yourself, try as you may.

Forming a Mastermind Alliance

Napoleon Hill likens a mastermind alliance to a top-notch airplane crew. You are the captain. You can take the plane to its destination only because all the other members of the crew recognize and respect your authority. Only because all of them know exactly where you are going, and only because they want to go there, too. And it works best when all enjoy the ride.

The conductor of a mastermind alliance has several jobs. The first is to know exactly where the plane is going and when it needs to get to its destination. Next, he or she needs to give clear, unmistakable directions to the crew. Each crew member needs to agree on the destination and time of arrival. Most importantly, each must be ready and able to do his or her assigned job.

The concept of the mastermind alliance worked to perfection when Ernest Bromley, Al Aguilar, and I got together to form Sosa and Associates, an advertising agency that grew to become the largest Hispanic agency in the United States (it is now called Bromley Communications and is still number one). Our goal was crystal clear: to become the largest and best Hispanic advertising agency in the country. We believed in this goal with all our hearts. Our belief was based on facts. In 1980, the Hispanic ad world was growing five times faster than mainstream advertising. We had only six competitors in the country. Best of all, there were dozens of Fortune 500 companies with big budgets wanting to explore this emerging market. "We can't fail," we reasoned. "All we have to do is work hard and smart to make it happen."

All three of us were riveted to the same opportunity. We agreed that we would, in fact, become the biggest and the best. Our minds had conceived. We believed. It was time to achieve.

Napoleon Hill's mantra, "Whatever your mind can conceive and believe, you can achieve," had become my mantra, too. In forming my mastermind alliance, I found that I had appropriated Hill's mind. In a very real sense, he was as much a part of the mastermind alliance as Sosa, Bromley, and Aguilar.

I drafted a plan on a napkin with big incentives for the three of us. Profits would be shared. Promotions would be given. Ernest and Al would become owners as we met our projected profit goals. Their names would be added to the agency's name when we became one of the top five ad agencies in the United States. When we met our goal of becoming number one, the plan was to sell 49 percent of our ownership to a prestigious worldwide firm. By doing so, we would become part of a global network of the most talented people in the business. My personal goal was to retire at age fifty-five and be financially secure for the rest of my life. When we drafted the plan, I was forty-five years old. We had just hatched a ten-year plan. On a napkin.

We made it happen in five!

That's because we believed. We worked long days, and many times weekends. We took the time to think things through.

We made the most of our strengths and worked around our weaknesses. For example, the three of us had ideas and opinions on just about everything. That was a strength as well as a weakness. Each of us was convinced we had the best idea on virtually every subject, especially Al and me. We knew this could become a big problem, so we made a deal: We divided responsibilities. Ernest would run the operations of the agency, media, and research. Al would be in charge of client services, positioning of the agency, and new business presentations. I would head the creative team and be the front man.

The decision to separate our responsibilities turned out to be critical. It kept us on track. It kept us sane. And it kept us out of each other's hair. When one of us had an idea, he shared it with the others, no matter how outrageous it was. We were free to give advice and counsel to each other's "department." However, only the person in charge of that department had the final say. After the decision was made, we all supported it fully and made it work.

Once a month on a Saturday, the three of us would meet at one of our homes to review, revise, and refine our plan. The meetings were about three hours long and very casual. Their purpose was to keep the plan in front of our eyes. We shared our plans and accomplishments with the agency at regular Monday morning meetings. As we grew, we had to move across the street to a hotel ballroom to hold them.

When I retired and left the agency, Ernest Bromley took over my position as chief executive officer. We agreed that the agency should have a new name. Bromley, Aguilar and Associates was

born. Now it was up to Mr. Bromley to form a new mastermind alliance to take the agency to its next level.

A new chemistry had to evolve. New responsibilities had to be
shared. New goals had to be generated. All of that took time as the
key individuals at Bromley began to reevaluate their own futures.
Al Aguilar left to form his own agency and his own mastermind alliance with his wife, Gisela. Adrienne Pulido, the chief operating
officer, left to start her own consulting firm and formed her own
mastermind alliance with her husband, Don.

For Ernest, forming a new mastermind alliance was to be a lot
more complicated than the first. Bromley Communications was
now part of Publicis, a giant French multinational. Ernest's new alliance now had to consider French executives as well as managers
of its other offices around the world. In the meantime, Bromley had
acquired a Miami-based agency with offices in Dallas and Los Angeles. The top-down Latin American management style of the
Miami-based agency was totally different from Ernest's open and
inclusive style. New executives in different cites, with different
backgrounds and management styles, had to function as one company. As one management team. As one mastermind alliance.

This was a big challenge for Ernest Bromley. Of course, he was
up to it. He put a new alliance in place by calling on his strengths.

Many years before, I had discovered that although I had started
Sosa and Associates, it was Ernest who kept it together. Ernest is a
natural manager. He combines all that is best in a partner, in a professional, in a boss, and in a human being. Having said this, his
most valuable asset is his ability to foster teamwork because people
trust him. Why do people trust him? First, because he's a good ad
man—he knows the business and doesn't make many mistakes.
Also, because he is fair, consistent, and calm. He is also an optimist.
Nothing rattles him. Even in times of chaos, he gives everyone the
feeling that everything's going to be okay. The guy is Mr. Cool.

Recently, he went before city hall to defend a big and prestigious contract, the San Antonio Convention and Visitors Bureau. I called him to see if I could help. He asked me to make a couple of calls on his behalf. The presentation was especially tough because city staff had recommended a competitor, not Bromley. We were to have lunch the next day, so I said, "Hope we can celebrate over champagne tomorrow."

"I hope so, too," he said. "But if not, we'll just cry over a beer." The account was extremely important to him and to his agency. Yet he did not treat it as a matter of life and death. He was calm and confident throughout the competitive process, and this in spite of the fact that he was running in second place.

When the final vote was cast, city council overruled staff. Bromley was reappointed by one vote, securing the seven-year, fifty-million-dollar contract. Yes, we were served champagne at lunch the next day.

Not every mastermind alliance works as well as the Sosa, Bromley, and Aguilar example. Others work even more smoothly and achieve much greater goals. The best example is that of Bill Gates, Paul Allen, and Steve Ballmer. These young men who started out in their parents' garages changed the way we work, learn, and live through the company they founded: Microsoft. It's made our lives easier. It's made information-gathering faster. In the process Gates became the richest man in the world, and Allen number four on the list. (By the way, it took me just twelve seconds to surf the Net to learn that Allen is number four. Ten years ago, it would have taken me a trip to the library, three hours, about $3.75 worth in gasoline, and $22.00 in wear and tear on my car.)

Again, their mastermind alliance worked because Gates, Ballmer, and Allen had a common goal—to put a personal computer within the reach of every individual and to make it easy for anyone to access the Internet. They also were smart enough to assign one another separate and distinct responsibilities, and they trusted each other to implement those responsibilities. They also agreed on the way that they would motivate and reward their people. The Microsoft alliance created an estimated ten thousand millionaires in the process! Not a bad example of the mastermind alliance at work. It is perhaps the world's best known.

Mastermind alliances are not restricted to business. The political world is full of examples. Bill and Hillary Clinton have weathered personal and political avalanches that would have buried most others, even the most astute. Yet, as of this writing, the two are popular, even admired multimillionaires who could well become the first husband and wife to each serve as U.S. president.

My personal favorite is the Bush family. I count them not only as my friends but also as my heroes. They have forged a political dynasty built on public service that I predict will be among the greatest and most enduring in American history. Their common goal is not personal gain but personal service. Whether you talk to George H. W., or Barbara, or George W., or Laura, or Jeb, or Columba, or even Jeb and Columba's son George P. Bush, you get the same sense of commitment to duty and country based on their mastermind alliance philosophy: that service to others is what makes public life in politics worth the effort.

In sports, Tiger Woods and his parents are a mastermind alliance. Tiger may hit the ball, but without his mother and father, he would be nowhere near the top of the game. The same is true of Venus and Serena Williams. At every one of their games, you can see one or both of their parents in the stands, either cheering or agonizing with every stroke their daughters take at the tennis ball. Like Tiger, they are champions. But only because they chose to get there as part of a mastermind alliance.

Musical groups and individual musicians come and go. Those who endure the longest are the ones who embrace a true mastermind alliance. The Rolling Stones are still touring and filling arenas after some forty-five years. Willie Nelson is on the road again, or, better said, on the road still after fifty-five years on tour. Tony

Bennett is another. All of them will tell you that they could have never done what they have done on their own.

But what about Latinos? There are plenty of examples. Julio Iglesias is the most popular recording artist in the world and has sold over 250 million albums worldwide. His sons Enrique and Julio Jr. are carrying on the tradition, breaking hearts with their music just as their old man did more than thirty years ago—and continues to do. Carlos Santana's music has found a whole new generation of fans, making him and his band as popular as they were in the 1970s. Gloria Estefan's star is shining as bright as ever after more than twenty-five years of recording in both English and Spanish. Her husband, Emilio, is not only her producer but also her greatest supporter. Their mastermind alliance includes a first-rate team of professional musicians, attorneys, and finance experts.

Today's generation of Latino personalities are as likely to have long and successful careers. Andy Garcia didn't stop with *The Godfather: Part III*. Salma Hayek will continue to produce, direct, and act in many more successful films after *Frida*. Penelope Cruz, Jennifer Lopez, Jimmy Smits, Edward James Olmos, and Alfred Molina are but a handful of many others who have the potential to become legends, too. Why? All of them understand that they did not achieve their success on their own. They also know that they will not stay on top all by themselves. Without the help of family, friends, and associates who form their mastermind alliance, each of their stars would cease to shine.

As you start to assemble your mastermind alliance, remember this story. Take time *at the beginning* to think about the people you will need to help you reach your goal. Think about their talent. Think about their personality. Are they optimists or pessimists? You don't want pessimists. They find problems, not solutions. Do they have a sense of humor? It really helps if they do. Humor defuses tension in stressful situations. Are they calm or frenetic? Calm people accomplish more. Frenetic people tend to make things seem harder than they really are. These personal qualities are essential to achieving success.

Do they agree with your goal? Do they have ideas that will improve or clarify your goal? Are they team players? Do they share your values? Do you like, really like, and respect them as people and as professionals? Do they believe in your goal so strongly that they will work as hard as you to make it a reality?

You don't have to assemble your entire team at once. In fact, most mastermind alliances start with two people and build from there. Also, don't be afraid to make changes if the team isn't clicking. Harmony, as Napoleon Hill observed, is key.

Whatever your age, whether twenty-three, as I was when my eyes were opened, or ninety-three, the sooner you put the mastermind alliance into practice, the sooner you will reach your goal.

Let's review the basics in forming your mastermind alliance:

- Make sure each member wants the exact same goal and will work as hard as you to make it happen. Write your goal down and sign your names to it. Reread your goal at least once a day.
- Agree to have each member of the alliance be responsible for a different aspect of the business. Put people in the slots that complement their talent and passion. Overlapping of responsibilities leads to problems.
- When you disagree, and you will on occasion, go with the decision of the person responsible. Then give 110 percent to make his or her idea successful. Never try to sabotage an idea that wasn't yours. People will notice and then work to sabotage yours. Your alliance will fall apart.
- Meet often, either formally or informally, to review how things are going. Daily is not too often. Communicate freely and openly. Build trust through trusting others.

- Work harder than the other members of the team. Never let them down. Always keep your word. The best partnerships are those in which every member of the team is convinced that the other members are contributing more than him or her.
- Believe in yourself and in your group. But when it's time for a member of your mastermind alliance to pursue other goals, it's okay. People change. So do alliances. Sometimes the right change makes things better.

One more bit of advice. If somebody ever tells you, "You can do anything you want," remember that they really mean, "You and your mastermind alliance can do anything you want."

4

An Attractive Personality
—Adrienne Pulido

The first time I came across Napoleon Hill's *The 17 Principles of Personal Achievement,* I was surprised to see "attractive personality" as the third-most important, yet it is. It was also surprising to learn that a pleasing personality has twenty-five qualities. I thought this was too many until I looked closer. Many of these qualities are closely related. Mr. Hill lists them as follows:

1. Positive mental attitude
2. Flexibility
3. Sincerity of purpose
4. Promptness of decision
5. Courtesy
6. Tact
7. Tone of voice
8. The habit of smiling
9. Facial expression
10. Tolerance

11. Frankness of manner and speech
12. A keen sense of humor
13. Faith in infinite intelligence
14. A keen sense of justice
15. Appropriate use of words
16. Effective speech
17. Emotional control
18. Alertness of interest
19. Versatility
20. Fondness for people
21. Humility
22. Effective showmanship
23. Clean sportsmanship
24. A good handshake
25. Personal magnetism

My wife, Kathy, and I are fortunate to know George W. Bush well. We have been part of his media team in three successive elections. "Dubya," as most Texans call him, is a natural leader. When you meet him and shake hands, he comes across just like your next-door neighbor. When you talk to him for a few minutes, his personal magnetism beams through. He can convince you to follow him anywhere. He is well aware of his leadership abilities and yet works to improve them every day.

A colleague of mine by the name of Adrienne Pulido has more than her share of these qualities. All of five feet tall in her high-heel shoes, she can dazzle team members and clients alike with her well-prepared, sparkling marketing presentations delivered with the skill and ease deserving of an Academy Award.

Adrienne came to work as a research assistant at Sosa and Associates straight out of college at the tender age of twenty-one. On her first day, my partner Al Aguilar asked her to accompany him to a focus group session that evening. A focus group is a session of ten to twelve people being interviewed together to give their opinions on various products and services. This particular group was to comment on a radio campaign we were developing for Burger King.

The next day, I asked her how it went. She said, "It was great! I learned a lot. But truthfully, the radio commercials we played for them are not very good."

"Did the groups hate them?" I asked.

"Not really," she smiled, "but I believe they were a bit *aburridos*, 'boring'—they can be better." Then she went on to suggest ways that the spots could be improved.

In two minutes on the second day at the job, Adrienne demonstrated the twenty-five qualities of an attractive personality. First, she had a positive mental attitude about everything. She was prompt in her decisions. She was courteous and tactful. She was frank in her speech. She used humor by inserting a Spanish word. She used appropriate words, even though a sharp critic. Her manner of speech was effective, to be sure. She was in perfect control of her emotions. She was alert and interested in the project. She showed a fondness for people. She was subtly humble in her approach. And she certainly demonstrated good sportsmanship and personal magnetism as she ended the conversation with a firm handshake and a sincere, "Thanks for the opportunity. This is going to be fun!"

Al couldn't believe what he had just seen. "We've got a winner on our hands," he said. Adrienne was a winner. Within a couple of years she was heading our research department, and in another few she was running the agency as vice president and head of operations. Today, Adrienne runs her own marketing consulting firm, carefully balancing her role as a professional, a mother of two, and the wife of a very supportive (and patient) husband, Don. She consults with companies large and small all over the United States and Latin America, advising them of future trends, especially as they relate to the Hispanic consumer market.

Positive Mental Attitude (PMA)

A positive mental attitude is the most important aspect of an attractive personality. It is an attitude of optimism—the feeling that everything is going to be all right, even when things look bad.

The first time I sat down to talk with George W. Bush about the strategy for his reelection campaign for governor in Texas, I asked him to describe himself as a leader. He said, "I'm an optimist. My attitude is always positive. You know why?" He didn't wait for my response. "Because people expect that in a leader. How many people do you think would follow me if I were a pessimist? Not many. A leader must have a positive mental attitude at all times."

It sounds so simple, but that's Dubya. He likes to make things simple and easy to understand. And whether you agree with his politics or not, you can almost feel the positive mental attitude he brings to the table.

Jimmy Carter was another good president. He won his first election with his positive, confident smile and optimistic outlook that were such a stark contrast to Gerald Ford and his connection to Richard Nixon and the Watergate scandal. Four years later, Carter lost his second term because he had changed. His bright smile had turned into a worried look. He made a speech in which he talked about the "malaise" that he thought was gripping America. Voters picked up on his pessimism and decided on a new president— Ronald Reagan—the man with a bigger smile and a more positive mental attitude.

Remember, you can't have the pleasing personality of a successful leader if you don't have a positive mental attitude.

Flexibility

Having a definiteness of purpose does not mean you never make changes. While keeping your eye on your goal, you must remain flexible. You may get a better idea. You may need to change a tactic because the competition got tougher, or because it rained on the day of your parade.

Several years ago, our ad agency was scheduled to make a big presentation in Washington, D.C. It was to be our first really big political account. Winning this business would put us on the map. In preparing for the presentation, we worked like never before. We prepared television storyboards, wrote radio commercials, and designed outdoor billboards. We practiced for three weeks and even memorized our parts. We conducted two dress rehearsals and perfected every prop.

On the day of the presentation, we took no chances. We got to the airport at 6 a.m.—two hours early. This was to be a five-hour flight from San Antonio through Houston and on to our nation's capital. All our presentation materials were checked in at the counter in plenty of time. We got to Washington on time. Our presentation didn't.

Panic attack!

We waited as long as we could at the airport, hoping that the airline would find our eight large boxes. It was not to be. Finally, when we could wait no longer, we got in a cab and went nervously on. As we neared the senator's office, a sense of calm came over us. "We'll just have to do the best we can—we have no other choice," we agreed.

We made the presentation without props. It turned out to be the best of our lives! The absence of props gave us a special energy that Senator John Tower and his staff of twenty people could feel. We won the business and we were on our way. I'll never forget the lessons I learned that day:

1. Keep sight of your goal.
2. Keep a positive mental attitude.
3. Be flexible—the situation may change.

Tower won reelection that year. Our ads made the difference. And our reputations as first-rate political consultants were solidified.

Sincerity of Purpose

You can't fake it. Either you're sincere in your definite purpose or you're not. Insincerity shows. Never kid yourself about that. You must care more for your customer and his success than you do for the fee he's paying you or for the prestige the assignment may bring.

Adrienne Pulido is a perfect example of sincerity of purpose. She takes on an assignment because it's what she wants to do, not what she has to do. She never puts the question of money first, although her clients are happy to pay her very well. Her questions are instead: Will I enjoy working with this person? Will I enjoy selling my client's product? Will I do everything possible to make my client successful? Will my client love what I do? Will I spend my client's money as if it were my own?" If the answer is yes to each of these, then she accepts the assignment.

Follow this principle and you'll be true to yourself. You'll love what you do, your sincerity will show naturally, and your personality will be even more attractive than it is now.

La sinceridad sale de dentro—no tiene receta, "Sincerity comes from inside—it has no prescription, no recipe."

Promptness of Decision

Few things are more unattractive than a person who consistently dillydallies. People who aren't prompt in their decisions miss deadlines. They break promises. They disappoint customers, colleagues, and staff. People assume they are nothing more than a *flojo*, a lazy and careless person. That's a Latino stereotype we can ill-afford to perpetuate.

Granted, sometimes decisions aren't easy. But somebody has to make them. If you're the leader, the decision will be yours. Don't be afraid to act. You'll make the correct decision more often than not. And getting it right *most of the time* will get you to your definite major purpose. You won't always be able to deliver everything you promised on schedule. But it's better to deliver 80 percent of it on time than to deliver 100 percent of it when it's no longer needed.

Successful people make decisions quickly. First, because they are confident about their definite major purpose. Second, because they have confidence in themselves. To build your confidence, make sure you know exactly *what* you want, when you want to get it, and exactly how much you'll earn when you get it. *How* you get there will come as if by magic! Remember, the *what* is infinitely more important than the *how*.

Courtesy

Courtesy is different from manners. Good manners can be taught. Courtesy comes naturally—from the heart. The good thing is, we all have courtesy in our hearts. All you have to do is cultivate it. It's a little like riding a bike: Once you learn, it stays with you because the ability is natural. If you never get on the bike, however, you will never make use of that innate ability.

Napoleon Hill says that courtesy is nothing more than respecting other people's feelings under all circumstances, the habit of going out of one's way to help the less fortunate.

At the San Fernando Cathedral in San Antonio, where 97 percent of all parishioners are middle- and lower-income Latinos, our friend and pastor, Father David Garcia, has found that more often than not his poorest parishioners are the most generous. I once saw an old woman, who was obviously very poor, put one hundred dollars in the hand of the archbishop, telling him to take it, so that he could help someone less fortunate than she.

It is often said that Latinos are friendly people. When people come back from visiting Mexico or Latin America, they always comment on the friendliness they experience. I think it's more than friendliness. Latinos are courteous by nature. And by custom. This is something we must continue to teach our children, and continue to pass on to everyone we meet.

Tact

There is a right moment and a wrong moment for everything. Successful people develop a knack for doing the right thing at the right time. Napoleon Hill made this observation in his study of truly successful individuals. He went on to say that tact is so closely associated with courtesy that you can't practice one without the other.

He went on to define the most common ways people show a lack of tact. I'll follow his outline, adding a few I believe apply to Latinos:

1. Dwelling on ills or misfortunes
2. Complaining about coworkers or bosses
3. Complaining about one's spouse or ex-spouse
4. Bragging endlessly about cute children, grandchildren, or pets
5. Gossiping, or *chismiando*
6. Taking home leftovers or centerpieces from parties, assuming it's one's right
7. Being *codo,* making a habit of never picking up the tab at a restaurant or bar
8. Borrowing CDs and videos from family and friends and being careless about returning them
9. Showing up uninvited or dropping in without notice
10. Making long-distance calls from another's phone or using someone's cell phone without asking

11. Changing the TV channel without asking others who are watching
12. Talking on the phone too long when simply chatting with a friend
13. Assuming that one's opinion is more important than others'
14. Believing one has the answer to practically everything, *presumiendo*
15. Speaking out of turn, *interrumpiendo*
16. Beginning every sentence with *yo,* "me"
17. Asking familiar questions in an attempt to appear closer to a person than one really is
18. Complaining when requests or favors are refused
19. Using bad or profane language
20. Telling off-color jokes
21. Correcting people in the presence of others
22. Declining requests from others in an arrogant manner
23. Openly questioning the soundness of others' opinions
24. Giving unsolicited advice, especially about family matters
25. Assuming one has the best idea most of the time

Few of us behave perfectly all of the time. If you catch yourself committing a breach of tact, correct it immediately. Apologize if you have offended someone with your behavior. Acknowledging an unintentional lapse is a sign of growth and maturity. We must work daily at perfecting a pleasing personality.

Tone of Voice

Have you ever seen yourself on a playback of a video, especially when you were unaware you were being taped? As you watched, did anything surprise you? Did you sound bossier than you intended?

Did you come off as less friendly or more silly? Was your voice as pleasant as you imagined?

Years ago, I videotaped a family vacation. In it, I was guiding two of my young children along a path in the woods. The camera was on them as they made their way. My voice was in the background. When I heard myself on the playback, I was astonished. "Watch out!" sounded mean, not helpful. *Cuidado,* "be careful," sounded bossy, not caring and concerned. I couldn't believe it. Was that me? Why did I sound so different?

Many times, we intend to say one thing, yet say another, simply because of our tone of voice. After playing that video a couple of times for my family, I asked my children if they thought I sounded mean and bossy. "Dad, you always sound that way."

Wow!

What a revelation. I had always thought of myself as a gentle, loving, helpful, protecting father, and here I was, being perceived as a mean *viejo,* "old man." Since that time, I have been much more careful with my tone of voice and have taped myself several times in an effort to improve. I must admit—it's painful. My progress was slow. Today, I take great care in saying exactly what I mean and how I mean it. I hope my family agrees with that (fingers crossed).

Facial Expression

Adrienne Pulido's facial expression is a perpetual smile. I can't ever remember her frowning or angry, no matter how tough the situation. It comes from an inner sense of confidence and thinking positive thoughts.

Your facial expression mirrors what you're feeling. Walking along the sidewalk, have you ever turned toward a mirror or seen yourself in a store window and suddenly caught yourself looking either happier or sadder than you thought? This is much like the example of the videotape playback I just mentioned. When you catch yourself unaware, you will see what others see.

It's almost impossible to hide pain, sorrow, anger, impatience, or any other negative emotion you may be feeling. That's why you must rid yourself of negativity by replacing it with positivity. Positive and happy thoughts will always be reflected by a beautiful facial expression—a must for a pleasing personality.

Tolerance

Abre los ojos y ve, "open your eyes and see." *Abre la mente y aprende,* "open your mind and learn." People who assume that everyone else should act like them, think like them, or be like them are unrealistic, immature, and naïve. The world of the twenty-first century is changing fast. New ways and new ideas are gaining dominance daily. Every community in every part of the country is becoming more diverse. Immigrants from other countries are working with us, living near us, and transforming our country and our world. We are exposed daily to new and different customs, religions, traditions, cultures, and languages.

Latinos are part of this wonderful change. If you are Latino, you want people to accept you. You expect equal treatment. You expect respect. The best way to get respect and acceptance is to give it. Many Latinos complain of discrimination though we discriminate against others.

Tolerance is accepting others' differences. Intolerance is a misplaced sense of importance. So is impatience. Tolerant people have the deep understanding of the importance of equality. Practice tolerance and patience. You will be richer for it.

Frankness of Manner and Speech

Remember Adrienne Pulido's second day on the job? She spoke her mind. She spoke out gently, with charm and grace, and with intelligence and professionalism. From the start, it was clear that she was an honest person, a forthright professional who could be counted on—and trusted. That's one of the reasons she rose to the top of her profession, running the country's largest Latino ad agency.

But let's not confuse frankness with off-the-cuff comments or carelessly expressed opinion. Some people blurt out the first thing that comes to mind without regard for whether it is appropriate or relevant. They are usually nothing more than show-offs. You would do well to ignore their comments. People who are not forthright cannot be counted on. They may not lie but they withhold information. According to Napoleon Hill, withholding information amounts to the same thing as a lie because it is basic dishonesty and undermines the soundest character.

Frankness is always appreciated. Especially when it's delivered as my friend Adrienne delivers it. Her grace and thoughtfulness enhance her pleasing personality.

A Keen Sense of Humor

Most successful people have a keen sense of humor. Humor goes a long way toward relieving tense situations and building teamwork. Take the relationship between men and women at the workplace. Many talented women don't get the promotions they deserve because they concentrate on the barriers they face and take themselves too seriously. This is also true of men. Constant seriousness can create unnecessary tension. Studies have shown that those who have risen to the top of the corporate world can laugh, joke, play tricks, and poke fun with best of them. Humor promotes a positive teamwork environment. It helps make life and work more fun and happy. Who doesn't want to be happy? If you aren't good at making jokes, that's fine. Just laugh at them.

Faith in Infinite Intelligence

Napoleon Hill was a great believer in the importance of faith in the achievement of any great undertaking. I couldn't agree more. Without faith, you can't direct your emotions and your inner being toward your definite purpose. You can't inspire others to follow you. Faith eliminates obstructions and inspires your creative mind toward finding new solutions when there seem to be none. It allows you to see past worldly obstacles. Faith enables you to keep on going when you think you are too tired to take another step, or to work another hour, or to lay another brick, or to type another word.

Faith in infinite intelligence unleashes the power within you. But remember, faith in infinite intelligence doesn't mean leaving everything up to God. It doesn't mean that a prayer on your knees or plea in the night will solve your problem. You must be part of the solution.

Faith is the inspiration that fuels your journey and enables you to accomplish your goal. The power of faith doesn't cost anything. No fee must be paid. It is yours for the taking. All you have to do is want to use it.

A Keen Sense of Justice

One of the most important attributes of a pleasing personality is the capacity to be fair, honest, and just. Even when it's not in your own best interests. A keen sense of justice means not showing favoritism. It means firing the person who's not performing. It means saying no to the wrong decision and standing up for the right one, even if it costs you money.

When Kathy and I were in business, our art director, Jeanette Mendez, was diagnosed with cancer at the age of twenty-nine. She had just gotten married and had her whole life in front of her. As she began her treatment, she became so weak she couldn't work for a year. We didn't have to call a special meeting to decide what to do. We kept her on at full salary. It was the right thing to do, the just thing. After all, she'd been with us for more than eight years. And she'd always given us her all, many times working all night to meet our deadlines. The least we could do was reciprocate.

The Appropriate Use of Words

It is important to use the appropriate language when communicating orally or in print. It's especially easy to get careless in your choice of words when speaking. Be careful that you are not engaging in confusing or incomplete communication.

When we put our message in writing, we tend to be more careful. This is because we become aware that whatever we write will be seen in print, where it could be questioned, or scrutinized. Mistakes, exaggerations, omissions, misstatements, and other flaws are more readily apparent. If our communication is sloppy, we won't have a leg to stand on.

It surprises me that so many people write hastily, carelessly, or unclearly. Do you? Take this test. Re-read the e-mails you've written over the past month with a critical eye. Pretend you're an English teacher. Is your communication as clear as it can be? Is it concise or does it ramble? Is it accurate? How many shortcuts did you take? How many misspelled words do you see? If you do not use clear and appropriate words to communicate in writing, chances are that you are not using them when you speak. By the way, we may think that curse words are expressive or effective. They are never appropriate.

You may have noticed that in my own writing, I use short sentences. And sentence fragments. That's because of my advertising background. In advertising you must get your point across in thirty seconds. It's also because I prefer to write the way I talk.

Effective Speech

"Don't ask what your country can do for you, ask what you can do for your country." Sounds funny, doesn't it? If John Fitzgerald Kennedy had delivered that line, no one would remember it today. I believe that he chose "ask not," instead of "don't ask," even though it's not the way we generally talk because he didn't want to start the sentence with a negative word. He wanted to be positive and inspirational.

You'll notice something else. Every word except "country" contains just one syllable. In fact, his entire inaugural address uses one-syllable words 90 percent of the time! Yet it is the most memorable and most quoted inaugural address in U.S. presidential history.

Some academicians cringe when I mention this. Some people prefer longer sentences and longer paragraphs with polysyllabic words. Big words impress some people. But most are not impressed. If you want words remembered (and who doesn't?), keep them simple.

Advertisers spend billions each year communicating their messages to their target audiences. They use the same principles John Kennedy used almost fifty years ago in his speech. They keep it simple. They keep it positive.

The following ad lines use one-syllable words. Can you guess the advertiser when the brand name is not part of the slogan?

It's the real thing.
Have it your way.
We love to see you smile.

Just do it.

Like a rock.

True.

Good to the last drop.

Tastes great—less filling.

This is your brain. This is your brain on drugs.

Be all that you can be.

Whazzup?

Get the door, it's Domino's.

SOME OLD ONES

I'd like to buy the world a Coke.

This Bud's for you.

If you've got the time, we've got the beer.

When you've said Bud, you've said it all.

We bring good things to life.

King of Beers.

ONLY ONE TWO-SYLLABLE WORD

Some things money can't buy.

You deserve a break today.

We try harder.

I'm lovin' it!

The one thing that advertisers do that John Kennedy didn't is borrow memorable familiar phrases to help us remember what they're trying to tell us.

When delivering a presentation or a speech, keep it simple. Keep it relevant. And keep it brief. Your audience is likely to remember what you said and remark, "I like that person!" It's all part of a pleasing personality.

Emotional Control

Much of what we do is directed by our feelings. When we feel good, we are more likely to do good things. When we feel bad, look out! Our feelings, wrote Napoleon Hill, can lift us to great achievements or hurl us down to defeat. We owe it to ourselves to understand and control our feelings.

He went on to identify seven negative and seven positive emotions. The seven negative ones are fear, hatred, anger, greed, jealousy, revenge, and superstition. These tend to surface when you get wrapped up in yourself—when you are thinking more about your own welfare than the welfare of others.

The seven positive emotions are love, sex, hope, faith, sympathy, optimism, and loyalty. Personally, I'm glad to see that sex made this list. Positive emotions tend to take the welfare of others into consideration. They are also noble.

Your emotions and the way you display them say a lot about you. People who don't care to control their emotions are usually quite selfish. They seem to think that the world revolves around them—that what they think, want to do, or say, is more important than what others think, do, or say.

Adrienne Pulido believes that people choose to do business with people because they are attracted to who those others are as human beings. "It's not about what you do, it's about who you are," she says. "It's the relationship that counts." Business relationships and personal relationships are built on emotion as much as anything else.

People are attracted to those who are positive, selfless, and care about others. They are repelled by negativity and selfishness. If your emotions are positive, your relationships will be positive. If you get careless and start to think more about yourself than about others, you will not be able to control your negative emotions. Your relationships, as well as your pleasing personality, are sure to go south.

Alertness of Interest

One of my grandsons had a habit of yawning when having a conversation with an adult, especially if it had to do with suggestions of improvements he might make. He wasn't aware of it, but it was a sure indication that he was not interested. One day, as he was rehearsing for a job interview, I counted ten yawns in ten minutes. I pointed this out to him. We then reversed roles. He quickly saw that my yawning while he was giving the interview was a big turnoff, a sure sign of lack of interest that couldn't be hidden.

One of the ways Adrienne Pulido gets new clients and keeps the ones she has is to stay interested in them, and in their business. She anticipates their needs. When she completes a project, she doesn't stop thinking about them. She keeps in touch and continues to be valuable. She sends them news articles relating to their business. She e-mails them her thoughts, ideas, and suggestions. She makes sure she doesn't forget them. In doing so, she isn't forgotten. She also keeps in touch with people who worked for her in the past. Some of her former employees have become clients, because she stays interested and alert.

Adrienne does favors without expecting anything in return. I am writing this book because she heard through one of her clients that the Napoleon Hill Foundation was looking for someone who could write it. She called and put me in touch with her client, who connected me to Don Green, the head of the foundation.

Fifteen years ago, I told Adrienne how *Think & Grow Rich* had changed my life. She remembered! So here I am, in a small hotel in the tiny town of Thaxted, England, just outside London, writing this chapter. I'm here because my wife is taking a course in French polishing. She's learning to restore antique furniture to advance her interior decorating business.

¡Qué vida! I love my life. Thank you, Adrienne, for your alertness, interest, *and good memory.*

Versatility

Versatility has always been an important component of a pleasing personality. And it is even more important today. One hundred and fifty years ago, a fellow could open up shop at age twenty-one and close it thirty or forty years later without ever having to expand his world of knowledge much. That was because the world was slow to change.

Today, the world changes every minute. So it is critical that you become aware of the changes happening around you. With today's computers and the Internet, it is easy and inexpensive to download anything you need to become thoroughly informed and versatile. As always, the more informed and versatile you are, the more interesting you become to successful people. The easier it then is to meet them, talk to them, and build friendships, which can lead to business opportunities. There's another bonus to versatility. It helps you better serve your community, as well as your family and friends.

Fondness for People

Dogs can tell whether or not you like them. If you like them, they like you back. In fact, they love you and will do anything they can to please you. People react the same way. If you don't like someone, chances are that they don't like you either.

Sometimes we make impulse judgments and dislike people without giving them a chance. Some white people dislike brown people just because they're brown. Some brown people dislike black people just because they're black. Fondness for people requires openness, maturity, and caring for others, no matter who they are, what they look like, or where they come from.

Muhammad Ali, perhaps the most recognized face in the world, has a natural fondness for all people, no matter who they are.

In his recent book, *The Soul of a Butterfly,* which he and his daughter wrote, he says:

> No matter where I go, everybody recognizes my face and knows my name. People love and admire me; they look up to me. That's a lot of power and influence to have, so I know I have a responsibility to use my fame in the right way. That's one of the reasons I've always tried to be good to everyone, no matter their color, religion, or position in life. Though other people may see themselves as better or more important than others, in God's eyes, we are all equal. It's what's in our hearts that matters.

What's in our hearts always shows. Keep your heart open to accept the best in everyone. Most everyone wants to be good. Most everyone wants to be fair. Most everyone wants to be liked. Give everyone the benefit of the doubt. Be fond of people and they will be fond of you.

Humility

Preaching humility to Latinos is like preaching prayer to the Pope. Latinos are humble by nature, by culture, and by history. I don't have to advise any Latino to remember to be humble. The only advice I can offer is to not overdo it. Know that you are no better and no worse than any other person. Napoleon Hill said that people who are strong in faith are always humble of heart, and that those qualities are always admired. Well said, Mr. Hill.

Clean Sportsmanship

Clean sportsmanship tends to occur naturally in an environment of trust. Trust doesn't come as naturally to Latinos as humility does. This is because so many of our forefathers were exploited for centuries. The conquistador killed, robbed, pillaged, and raped the indigenous people. The Indians learned to be leery. And to take from the rich before the rich took from them. Soon everyone was robbing everyone else. *Me los tengo que fregar antes de que me frieguen,* "I've got to get them before they get me." Trust went out the window, and so did clean sportsmanship.

I'm not implying that Latinos today don't play fair. We do. We must, however, work a little harder on learning to trust. Especially to trust people who are different from us. Trust is built on friendships—on our getting to know one another. So go out of your way to get to know other people. Once you know them, you are much more likely to like them. If you like them, you are more likely to trust them.

Most people are trustworthy. *Trusting everyone is better than trusting no one.* If you assume that most everyone is trustworthy, you will not only have a pleasing personality, you will also be a good and fair sportsman.

A Good Handshake and Personal Magnetism

When you shake someone's hand, always look them in the eye. Never look down. Smile. Shake hands warmly, not too hard, not too soft. "Glad to see you again," "Good to meet you," and "Wonderful to make your acquaintance" are the expected greetings. Use them with gusto. These days, the warm *abrazo* is cool, so go ahead and offer a hug. Even to Anglos you are meeting for the first time, what the heck? They will be more likely to remember you. And your *abrazo.*

Personal magnetism is a quality people are born with. It has something to do with sexual energy. Julio Iglesias has it. So does Bill Clinton. Christina Aguilera has it and so does Jennifer Lopez. I've met both Clinton and J-Lo and can tell you that the power of their magnetism comes through. Napoleon Hill noted long ago, that sexual energy is a driving, universal force. Channel its energy into your efforts. Make your efforts, not your body, the source of appeal to others.

So there you have it. The twenty-five traits of a pleasing personality. You may never perfect them all, but you can work to improve them all. Know which ones need your attention. Review them from time to time and make note of your improvement.

Building a pleasing personality is a lot like building a strong body with big muscles. It takes hard and consistent work to see improvement. But the longer you stay with it, the more improvement you'll see.

5

Applied Faith
—Jesse Treviño

Faith comes naturally to Latinos. It's in our hearts as well as in our language. We don't really say goodbye. Our *adiós* is the contraction of the two words, *A Dios,* or "To God." *Vaya con Dios* literally means "Go with God." We easily use the phrase *Que Dios te bendinga,* "May God bless you," when parting. When someone makes a wish, the common response is *Que Dios te lo conceda,* "May God grant it."

Debes tener fe, "You gotta have faith," is our call to action when the going gets tough. So is *En la lucha,* or *La lucha sigue.* Those translate into "In the fight," or "The fight goes on." Every day, consciously and unconsciously, we Latinos express our faith. It's who we are. The question is, how well do we apply our faith in our everyday lives?

Napoleon Hill cautions that it is not enough to have faith. He emphasizes that you must *use* it. "Faith is a state of mind, not necessarily your religious beliefs," he says. "For faith to be useful to you in achieving *lasting* success, it must be an active, not a passive faith."

Successful people know this: The faith you act on is the only useful faith there is.

I describe useful faith as a faith based on three critical truths: a belief in yourself, a belief in your goal, and a belief in infinite intelligence.

Understanding Infinite Intelligence

Mr. Hill teaches that it is impossible to apply your faith without a belief in a Supreme Being. I agree. The power of the Supreme Being is always at our side, waiting to give us a helping hand whenever we need it. When we draw on that power, we are drawing on the power within ourselves. The power of infinite intelligence is in every one of us. In the last chapter of this book, you will learn what many people don't know—we can't separate ourselves from the power of infinite intelligence. How else would we, as mortals, be able to consistently achieve all we can conceive?

Overcoming Disbelief

Mr. Hill says that having faith means relaxing your own reason and willpower and opening your mind to the power of infinite intelligence. If you truly believe in your definite major purpose, you can let faith take over and show you the way. It won't do the work for you. But it will point you in the direction you need to go. Faith will solve the seemingly unsolvable. It will magically open doors of opportunity you never knew were there. It will miraculously put the very thing you are looking for right in front of you.

Faith is believing in your dream. Without hesitation or reservation. Faith gives you the courage to keep focused and to keep going even when the going gets tough. All you must do is believe. If you don't believe, you can't put the power of faith to work for you.

The Power of Faith

One of the best-known Latino artists in the country is the great painter and muralist Jesse Treviño. His works hang at the Smithsonian Institution's American Art Museum in Washington, D.C. His large oil-on-linen paintings grace the homes and offices of influential collectors. A massive 100-foot-tall mural by Jesse is the picture-perfect backdrop for a children's park in downtown San Antonio. His passion for public art is legendary, as are his faith and courage.

In the late 1990s, Treviño accompanied First Lady Hillary Clinton on an art tour to Santiago, Chile, where she introduced him as her favorite artist. Later, she invited him to Washington, where he spoke before a group of art lovers and patrons of the arts at the White House. His career is remarkable, especially when you consider that Jesse was one of twelve children who grew up in poverty in a single-parent household. It is even more remarkable when you consider that Treviño achieved his greatest fame as an artist after losing his painting hand while serving on active duty in Vietnam.

Through applied faith, he achieved his definite major goal of becoming a prominent and respected artist, in spite of the odds against him. His story is an inspiration to us all. *Este es un hombre que tiene fe,* "this is a man who has faith."

Jesse Had the Power of Faith as a *Niño*

Even as a boy of five, Jesse loved art, especially art that was out in public for everyone to enjoy. He would spend hours watching artists hand-painting giant commercial billboards. To him that was art. He marveled at their control of each brushstroke. They could paint faces. They could paint cars. They could paint food. They could even paint letters. "How wonderful it must be to be able to do that," he thought to himself. "One day, I'll paint just like they do."

Having faith came naturally to Jesse. From that moment on, he always had the belief and the faith that he would be a great artist one day. He never imagined obstacles getting in the way of his goal. He woke up every morning thinking about art. He went to bed each evening dreaming about it.

A few blocks from home was a small lake where Jesse and his brothers went fishing in the summer. Right behind it stood Our Lady of the Lake University. Magnificent in its architecture, the institution had been built a hundred years before. As he waited for the fish to bite, Jesse would stare at the beautiful Gothic edifice. Something about it seemed to beckon him. Years later he would walk across its stage, smiling and proudly waving his college diploma above his head.

When Jesse was ten, a heart attack took his father's life at the age of forty-nine. The twelve siblings and their mother were left to fend for themselves. The older ones went to work, as did the feisty Mrs. Treviño. The family grew closer than ever, and, in their grief, they drew strength from each other. Jesse and his mother became closer. She was his best friend, and busy as she was, always found time to sit down and share her wisdom with him and his eight brothers and three sisters. *Tenemos fe,* "We have faith," became the family prayer.

Faith they had. Without coaching, Jesse began to apply it. Two big things motivated him. First, his mother's fondest wish: that one day her children would go to college. Second, his desire to earn recognition *and* money through his art. As early as age six, he began to win art contests. In the first grade, he won first prize in a drawing promotion sponsored by the biggest and most important museum in town. His pencil drawing of a dove on manila paper won him a forty-dollar savings bond, a plaque, and best of all, a standing ovation by an admiring audience. As the crowd stood and applauded,

Jesse was overcome with pride and joy! "This is the way I want to feel all the time," he remembers thinking.

After that experience, he entered every art contest he could find. Jesse had faith in his talent, and he applied it. He was tireless. Not a day went by when he was not drawing, painting, or reading art books. He entered and won contest after contest. By the time he was a senior in high school, his talent and discipline were well-known and respected.

But Jesse needed more. His definite major purpose was becoming clearer every day. He would become a famous artist and he would earn a lot of money. To do that, he knew he would need more schooling. He had to find a way to earn a scholarship to a world-class art school. Jesse's high school commercial art teacher, Katherine Aslup, came to the rescue. She had studied fashion art at the prestigious Pratt Institute. She was a fantastic artist who could work in any medium from pencil to pastels to oil. She also had great faith in her young student. She encouraged Jesse to enter a national art contest sponsored by *National Scholastic Magazine*. The prize? A fully paid scholarship to a first-class art school!

To win, Jesse knew his portfolio would have to catch the attention of the judges. Sheer talent wasn't enough. He wanted to stand out by being bold and different. With careful coaching, Jesse prepared a portfolio consisting of twenty pieces. Each was a drawing or painting of the face of a child. Each was rendered in a different medium: watercolor, oil, pastel, pencil, and pen and ink. Once again, Jesse was backing up faith with action. He didn't just wish it. He didn't just want it. He worked hard and remained positive. He went the extra mile. He stayed focused on his main definite purpose. He won the contest.

His applied faith paid off. He was offered a fully paid scholarship at two of the most prestigious art schools in the country. He could choose between the Chicago Art Institute and the Art Students' League of New York. He chose New York. Life was grand in the big city, even though it took the eighteen-year-old a few weeks to adjust. He went to school by day and to work by night. Every evening, six days a week, at a small sidewalk art shop in Greenwich Village, he drew pencil portraits of tourists for twenty dollars each. Jesse was very good. He could draw a nice crowd when he sketched, so the owner decided to place him up front for all to see.

Once people saw his work, they couldn't resist. His take-home was great: Jesse got fifteen dollars for every drawing. The shop owner took five, and made his real money on the frames. Every evening Jesse took home a hundred-fifty to two hundred dollars, a fortune to a young man in the mid-1960s. Life was good. In fact, perfect.

Overcoming Fear

One day, out of the blue, came the dreaded Greetings telegram from Uncle Sam. The Vietnam War was raging, the draft was on, and young men were being called to active duty. "Report in three days to your local draft office in San Antonio."

"¿Qué pasa? What's happening?"

Jesse had known that there was a war going on, of course. But he had been so preoccupied with his schooling and his job, he hadn't really thought much about it. Now, he'd be in the middle of it, a foot soldier in the U.S. Army. As soon as he got to camp, he put in for a job as a combat artist, where he could exercise his talent. There was no such job to be had. Television was covering the war now and there was no demand for the drawings that had helped chronicle past wars. So on to infantry training he went.

After a few weeks of basic training, Jesse was sent to fight in the killing fields of the Mekong Delta. In just three months, half of his company had either been killed or wounded. It was getting scary. Fear was in the air. "It felt like it was just a matter of time before I got mine," Jesse remembers.

Jesse's fear of death was real. It is the scariest fear of all. We'll explore the fear of death—listed as the last of the seven basic fears—later in this chapter. Napoleon Hill discovered that most of us suffer from at least one of these seven. My experience tells me that most Latinos suffer from multiple crippling fears. Not because we are *gallinas,* "chickens," but because of our cultural conditioning.

Here are the seven fears. Are any of these familiar to you?

The First Fear: Poverty

Many Latinos, me included, were taught to believe that poverty is a virtue. Our parish priest preached it from the pulpit on Sundays. Many times our own parents, family, and friends emphasized it. They would have us believe that the poor are all God-fearing saintly people on the road to heaven. Wealthy people, they believed, were miserable, wretched souls destined to go straight to hell. If a Latino becomes rich, it is often assumed he is dealing in drugs or some other underhanded activity. These cultural stereotypes have no connection with reality.

Speaking of reality, the fear of poverty is as real and as destructive as the unconscious acceptance of poverty. If we were taught that poverty is the road to heaven, wouldn't we all want to go there? If you resent poverty and want to get rid of it, analyze the negatives it creates the way Napoleon Hill did:

Avoidance of ambition. Lo que Dios quiera, "Whatever God wants." Is this your way of accepting whatever life hands you without challenging it? Remember, a happy successful life is as much up to you as it is to God.

Failure to make your own decisions. Como Dios quiera, "however God wants it." This attitude is a close relative to avoidance of ambition. It gives you permission to let outside forces determine what happens to you. It undermines the most precious thing the Creator gave you—your free will.

Making excuses for your failures. "It wasn't meant to be." Giving up and calling it a sign from God is the least acceptable excuse for failure. If you fail, you must learn from it, fix it, and try again. Accept the fact that you are responsible for what happens to you.

A negative mental attitude. A famous saying in Spanish is *Lo que será, será,* "whatever will be, will be." Another is *Ni modo,* "what's the use?" Both are meant to be wise and truthful sayings. In reality, they are quite the opposite, because they reinforce all the limitations that poverty brings.

The Second Fear: Criticism

As a young girl, Sandra Cisneros—author, lecturer, and writer—had a fear of being criticized by the nuns who were her teachers in school. When she changed schools in the third grade, the new teachers (also nuns) were different. Instead of teaching through fear and intimidation, they taught through love, encouragement, and understanding. These nuns recognized her talent and nurtured it.

From then on, Sandra felt compelled to try her hardest just to please them. The new school changed her life. Had she stayed at the first one, she would not be a writer today. Sandra lost her fear of criticism at a very young age.

Good thing. Napoleon Hill observed that a fear of criticism might lead us to do some very unnecessary things:

Keeping up with the Joneses or the Garcias. Trying to be the coolest, most sophisticated person on the block. The one with the snazziest car, the biggest media room, or the latest computer. This nonsense can cripple you, both emotionally and financially.

Bragging about your achievements. Yo ya fui y vine, a "been there, done that" attitude is a way of covering up feelings of inferiority, Hill says. If you pretend to have success rather than actually attain it, you will be crippled by the prospect of exposure as a fraud. If you work hard and take pride in your accomplishments, your achievements will speak for themselves.

Being easily shamed. Que vergüenza! is a common Mexican expression. Many of us are taught that shame is a desirable quality that keeps you in line. As Latinos, we've all heard the expression, *No tiene vergüenza,* "He has no shame," as if having shame would make him a better person. Shame causes you to doubt your decisions, to fear meeting people, and to lack self-confidence. You don't want to live in the fatalistic mindset of the *pobre, chaparro, y feo,* "poor, short, and ugly." This self-perception is painfully self-defeating. It can also become a reality if you let it.

The Third Fear: Ill Health

Latinos are at higher risk for certain diseases like diabetes and heart disease. A lot of our people are overweight. Many of us don't have adequate health insurance. And most of us hate going to the doctor.

The macho man. Many a Latino macho man has come close to death before seeing a doctor. A carpenter I know was bitten by a brown recluse spider and held off going to the doctor until he was in such pain that he had no choice. Had he rushed to the hospital right after the bite, he would have gotten the proper medication and spent a couple of days recovering. Instead, he lost the function of some of his vital organs, several months of work, and his life's savings. He also caused his family much pain and suffering. Today, he could be a strong healthy man. Instead, he is permanently handicapped, barely able to get through the day. All because he thought he could hide his fear by pretending to be "a real macho man."

I'd rather not know. Many of us are so afraid of getting sick, we think we can avoid illness by avoiding doctors and hospitals altogether. "If it's my time to go, it's my time. I don't want to go to the doctor, he might tell me I'm sick." That kind of thinking will make you worry even more, or even worse, will allow you to dwell in self-pity, creating havoc for everyone around you.

The habit of substance abuse. The daily *cervezita* after a hard day's work can become a habit. The "night out with the boys" can do the same. Whether it's drink or drugs, Napoleon Hill observed that substance abuse is nothing more than a cover-up for a fear of some physical or mental pain. You must seek out the source of that pain and address it. We'll cover this in greater detail in chapter 15.

The Fourth Fear: The Loss of Love

I know a man (let's call him Frank Mena) who suddenly lost his wife and family one day. Not to death, but to the fear of the loss of love. Frank is a good man and as smart as they come. The Menas appeared to be the perfect family. He had his own successful business. His wife was a homemaker: beautiful, talented, and social. His children were smart, polite, and attractive. He loved them so much that the thought of losing them was often on his mind. To make sure they stayed together, he hovered over them, dictating their every move.

One day, his wife came to him and said, "I'm leaving you."

"Why?" he asked in astonishment.

"I don't love you anymore."

"Of course you love me. Get real!"

"I said, 'I don't love you anymore,' " she repeated.

His reply? "You know you love me and I love you. You'll come to your senses. You can't leave me. I've given you everything you could possibly want. Go back inside the house and get ready. I'm taking you out to dinner. I don't want to talk about this anymore."

She didn't get ready for dinner. She left and never came back.

That was more than twenty years ago. My friend has never re-married, forever fearing the loss of love again. Frank really loved his wife. I suspect he adores her to this day. But he didn't listen. He overcontrolled. He feared losing love and tried too hard to guard against it.

Living in fear of losing love is living a nightmare. One that could become a reality if you obsess over it. Napoleon Hill advises us to cultivate our relationships. Give them your all. Instead of being a source of fear, each relationship will then be a bastion of strength and courage for you.

The Fifth Fear: Old Age

Our oldest daughter, Anna, is forty-four years old. She is beautiful, as are all our four girls. She, however, is convinced she's the prettiest. The other day she noticed the first wrinkles on her hands and was a bit distressed about it. Being a senior citizen myself, I understand the physical changes that take place as one progresses on the journey of life.

"I'm getting old," she said.

"That's okay," I replied, borrowing a phrase I had just heard days before. "If you wanna keep on livin', you gotta keep on aging." She didn't like the ditty but agreed that she wants to keep on living. Truth is, age is what you make it. You can decide to be old at thirty, forty, or fifty. You can also decide to be young at sixty-five, eighty-five, or ninety-five.

If you're gonna keep on livin', you're gonna keep on aging. As my friend Jose Martinez always says, "If it's going to happen, be for it." Aging is happening to me. So I'm for it!

Living is a good thing. Think of it that way and you will live a long, healthy, and happy life. Today's medicine is helping us live much longer, so take good care of your body no matter what your age is. There's a whole chapter devoted to health in this book, so I won't get into it here, other than to give you my four rules for staying healthy:

1. Love your work. If you don't love it, quit.
2. Stretch, lift weights, and walk a mile a day.
3. Drink eight glasses of water each day.
4. Eat small meals and never weigh more than fifteen pounds more than you did in high school.

The Sixth Fear: Loss of Liberty

Most of us believe that every human being yearns for freedom no matter where he or she lives. Napoleon Hill certainly did. He wrote on this subject more than seventy years ago and I marvel at how relevant his words are today. So I'll repeat them:

> No matter where you live in any country, the fear of the loss of freedom is present. For those suffering in police states, rather than enjoying the liberty that Americans possess, the fear is great. But many other forces can work to limit your freedom—the political ambitions of your neighbors, the demands on your daily life. These fears can paralyze you and distract you from your major definite purpose.
>
> The only way to fight this fear is to take an active role in defending the institutions that preserve your liberty. The rights we enjoy in this country were won through bitter years of struggle and can be maintained only by constant vigilance. You must be aware of the struggles that are taking place and take an active part in them and you must also be sure that you are doing nothing that encroaches upon the liberties of others.
>
> If you become a tyrant in the pursuit of your definite major purpose, seeking to dominate your family, your mastermind alliance, or your employees, you will

be rolling back the cause of freedom just as certainly as does any revolutionary extremist. You cannot be free of this fear yourself, if you are not in harmony with the very forces of liberty which make your own success possible.

The Seventh Fear: Death

This is the mother of all fears. Jesse Treviño certainly experienced it. He didn't die, and neither have we, so we don't really know what death is like. But if we fret and worry over it, it can literally kill us. It almost killed my brother Robert.

Robert got stomach cancer a few years ago. He was given a 5 percent chance of survival. As he went through his radiation and chemotherapy treatments, he became very ill and began to obsess about his illness. It was all he could think about or talk about. My wife Kathy advised him to go to the best therapist in town, a fellow by the name of Irv Loev. Robert's weight was down from 165 to 123 pounds. He had even begun planning his funeral. Yet he took Kathy's advice and went to see Irv. When he got to the doctor's office, Irv asked, "What's the problem?"

"I've got cancer and all I can do is think about it. It's killing me!"

"Well then, stop thinking about it," said Irv.

Robert, not one to spend time or money unnecessarily, took Irv's advice immediately. He didn't need to go back for months of therapy. He just stopped thinking about his illness. Right then and there. He got well.

Today, Robert is healthy and living a full and happy life. He and I paint on Sundays along with our friend Oscar Vaca. My brother learned well. He stopped thinking about death. Best of all, he stopped fearing it.

Demonstrating the Power of Your Faith

Jesse Treviño experienced the worst of the seven basic fears, the fear of death. As he watched his buddies die around him in Vietnam and continued to see firepower aimed his way, he feared the worst. Then it happened. Walking back from a search-and-destroy mission, he set off a booby trap and was blown forty feet into the air. He landed facedown in a swampy rice paddy. His right leg was twisted around the other side of his body. His right arm was on fire and almost severed at the elbow. It was spewing blood and dangling from his upper arm. The main artery in his leg was cut in half. He couldn't move. He was bleeding to death.

Private First Class Treviño survived thanks to the quick action of his buddies, who dragged him to a helicopter and flew him to a M.A.S.H. field hospital. They patched him up and saved his life. In a few days he was back in San Antonio at the Brooke Army Medical Center—where he would spend the next two years recuperating.

Those two years in bed, unable to move, were both a curse and a blessing to Jesse. On the one hand, his immobility made him angry. His right hand was gone. It bred despair. Would he ever paint again? What would he do with his life? It seemed to be over.

On the other hand, it gave him plenty of time to think. His mother had visited him every day for the two full years. Sometimes they wouldn't talk, but she was there. He thought about the really important things in his life. "If I could paint again, what would I paint?"

Then he had an epiphany. "If I learn to paint all over again with my left hand, I will paint the things I love the most—my family and my neighborhood!" His faith returned and he vowed to start all over again.

He took classes with beginning artists at the junior college. He painted murals of the horrors of war across his bedroom walls. He painted a giant canvas at Our Lady of the Lake University. He got his master's degree. Then he made the biggest discovery of all. The challenge of learning to paint all over again was not as tough as he thought. The talent and knowledge needed to paint was in his head. In his mind. In his heart. Not his hand. It had been there all along!

Jesse was strong enough to overcome defeat by developing a definiteness of purpose built on faith. And he applied it. He created images of success in his mind. He conceived of being an artist. Then he believed he would be an artist. And finally, he achieved his dream of being one.

Whatever your mind can conceive and believe, it can achieve. Hill's mantra is based on faith in one's own ability to achieve success. You can believe it or not believe it. Without faith, you will dismiss this great truth. With faith, it becomes truth and changes your life.

Developing a definiteness of purpose is the first step toward replacing a negative mental attitude with a positive one. If Jesse had given up while lying helplessly in that hospital bed, he might have succumbed to negative and hopeless feelings. Today, he's convinced he would not have become the influential and respected artist he is had he not stepped on that booby trap. That instant changed his life. For the better.

In his climb to the top of the artistic world, Jesse Treviño has had his highs and lows to be sure. It has not been an easy journey. Yet he has kept the faith. Although he came close to losing hope several times, something inside kept him going. That something was his faith. And his ability to apply it.

The Extra Mile
—Alberto Gonzales

Going the extra mile or doing more than people expect you to do is an amazing idea. When applied with the right attitude, it will produce explosive results almost immediately—*una inmediata explosión de resultados.* As far as I'm concerned, it is one of the most important principles in Napoleon Hill's philosophy. Over the years, it is one of the four I've truly mastered. The three others are positive mental attitude, definiteness of purpose, and mastermind alliance. I even gave them a name: "The Big Four Windows to Success," *las Cuatro Ventanas al Éxito.*

If you master these four, the other thirteen will naturally fall into place. Your conscious and subconscious minds will accept them as truth, allowing you to capture the magic and attain your definite major purpose on schedule. There isn't a day that goes by that I don't think consciously about applying them. They are mine for the taking. You can remember them using this memory jogger: P for positive, P for purpose, M for mastermind, and M for mile—PPMM.

Napoleon Hill describes going the extra mile as: "Rendering more and better service than what you are paid to do and doing it consistently with a positive mental attitude." Do this, he says, and you will receive compound interest on your investment. It's another way of saying, "Give and you will receive."

Let's examine Hill's principle closely. It has a compound expectation of you.

1. Do more than you are expected to do.
2. Do it every day.
3. Do it happily.

It also has a compound reward.

1. You will get back all you give.
2. Many times over.

I could end this chapter now and say, "That's all you need to know. Follow these three steps and you'll see the magic happen." But if I did that, you wouldn't get to savor some of the best and most dramatic stories of how this principle can change your life.

Amaze Your Friends and Bosses

During the fifth week at Mr. Hill's School of Personal Achievement, I learned the principle of going the extra mile. It was a lesson I never forgot. "Do more than you are expected to do. Do it every day. Do it with a smile." Because the promise of reward was so great, I decided to give it my all: I would work two extra hours a day at no extra pay at my minimum wage job as a sign painter at Texas Neon Sign Company on Josephine Street in San Antonio. I did just that five days a week. For a whole year. I did it with a big smile on my face.

After a couple days of staying late at the plant, my supervisor came over and asked, "Who authorized this overtime?"

"This is not overtime, Mr. Tripp," I said. "I punched out at 4:30. I'm just gonna work two extra hours a day every day for a year."

"Why?"

"I want to get rich."

"You think you'll get rich by working for nothing?"

"Napoleon Hill said I would get rich by doing more than is expected of me." I smiled and returned to my work.

Mr. Tripp just shook his head. He must have thought, "This kid is weird." Yet he encouraged me even as he questioned my sanity. Each day at about 6 p.m., he waved good-bye as he left the plant. "Be sure to lock up and turn the lights off, okay?"

I used the two extra hours to design and build wooden forms to manufacture custom raised-plastic letters. No one else in town was doing it, so the three-dimensional custom-made plastic sign was a breakthrough, a Texas Neon Sign Company exclusive. We could duplicate logos, pictures, and any lettering style imaginable in three dimensions! We sold all the custom signs we could make. We outsold our competition for several years before they caught up to us. I got a raise. Then another. And another. Soon I was earning almost as much as fellows who'd been at the job for twenty years. The competition offered me an even better position. I took the offer but was coaxed back by Jim Ryan, the owner, who gave me a deal I couldn't refuse—another raise. And my own office.

If you do more than people expect of you, you will stand out in the crowd. You will be noticed. You will be talked about. You will get ahead sooner. That's true because so few people are willing to put forth the effort it takes to go the extra mile every day. In fact, many people do quite the opposite. They habitually do as *little* as they can to get by.

The Alberto Gonzales Phenomenon

Attorney General Alberto Gonzales is an unassuming man. Totally unpretentious and down to earth. If you met him outside Washington, say, at your kid's soccer game and didn't know who he was, you might think he was the school science teacher or the principal. The first time I met him was at a Texas A&M football game at College Station five years ago. During halftime I turned and noticed him. He was sitting alone, happily munching on a bag of peanuts while dozens of Aggies all around him busily networked with one another. Alberto was not a public figure then, even though his job was big. He was a Texas State Supreme Court judge and had already served as Texas secretary of state.

He looked familiar but I couldn't place him. So I went over to introduce myself. "Hello, I'm Lionel Sosa," I said, extending my hand. "I know who you are," he said with a slight grin. "You helped with the governor's advertising campaign. I like your work."

"Thanks," I replied, "and you are?"

When he told me his name, I was embarrassed. Being both a fellow Latino and Texan, I should have known. Everyone else there did. "Sorry," I apologized.

Alberto, being a gentleman, took no offense. We chatted briefly about his job and politics. Those few minutes of conversation gave me an insight into the man. He is smart. He is aware of everything and everyone around him. He is a quick study and not particularly fond of small talk. He is a man on a mission. A mission of focusing on the job at hand. Of being the best at what he does.

Since then, I learned that he has come as far as he has by applying the principle of going the extra mile. He truly does more than is expected of him. And he does it every day in his own quiet way. He is a low-key person who prefers to let his high-profile actions speak for themselves.

Humble Roots and Big Dreams

The second of eight children, Alberto was born in San Antonio to parents who dropped out of school before they finished the sixth grade. He grew up in a two-bedroom house in Houston, where his parents still live. His father always stressed education as a way to learn a trade, not as a path to any diploma or degree. College wasn't on the family radar screen back then. Working hard and doing more than people expected them to do was. *Trabajo duro es honor,* "There is honor in hard work."

At twelve, when many kids his age were playing games, Alberto was hard at work, doing more than expected. At nearby Rice University stadium, he sold soda pop, peanuts, and popcorn on weekends. As he walked through the ivy-covered, tree-shaded campus he began to wonder, "Maybe this is where I belong . . . What if? Probably not . . . but who knows?"

Somehow, his very presence on the beautiful and peaceful campus, watching the proud and success-driven students confidently making their way from class to class, made a big impression on him. He began to imagine himself as one of them. His fantasy seemed impossible at first. Still, he couldn't help but dream.

In high school, he took tough courses and earned his diploma. His parents were enormously and completely proud when he graduated. It was so much more than they had achieved. The family tradition of working hard and going the extra mile was now being focused in a new direction: education. It just wasn't apparent quite yet.

Right out of high school, Alberto and a high school buddy joined the Air Force. There they reasoned they could make a living while learning a trade. The Air Force required all enlistees to complete an assignment away from their home base. So, after basic training, he chose a stint at Fort Yukon, Alaska, sixty miles north of the Arctic Circle. He didn't know it at the time, but it turned out to be the opportunity of a lifetime.

There were only one hundred GIs at Fort Yukon. Two of them had attended the Air Force Academy. Those two saw something in Alberto: In addition to his talent and intelligence, he had the habit of working harder and longer than anyone expected. Alberto went the extra mile at every opportunity. He had what it took to excel as an Air Force officer. The two academy graduates began to encourage him to seek an appointment. Soon all chipped in to help. From writing letters to congressmen, to flying him to an Army post to get his physical, to arranging for a proctor to come from Anchorage to administer the ACT and SAT tests, everyone got into the act. And when it was said and done, he received the appointment.

Now he had the opportunity to prove himself at one of the nation's most elite institutions of higher learning: the Air Force Academy. After two years of intensive physics and military history there, his dreams of becoming a pilot gave way to dreams of the law. He applied for a transfer and was accepted to Rice University, the very place where just a few years before he had been a peanut vendor. He found himself a student at the very university where his thoughts of university began.

After graduating with honors from Rice, Alberto had his choice of law schools. Harvard gave him the opportunity to live in the Northeast and test himself against the brightest legal minds in the country. Upon graduation, he was recruited by the Houston law firm of Vincent and Elkins. In 1995, he became one of the first of two minorities to make partner.

Alberto couldn't sit still. He looked for a new challenge. The habit of going the extra mile was a part of him, just as it had been a part of his parents' work ethic. Now he wanted to take his career in a new direction, one that would help people's lives. The new governor of Texas, George W. Bush, would give him that opportunity, and their association would make history.

Alberto became the governor's top legal advisor during Bush's first term. Bush then named him Texas secretary of state in 1997, and appointed him to the Texas Supreme Court in 1999. When Bush became president, Gonzales was asked to serve as White House Counsel, advising the president on all legal issues concerning the Executive Office of the President and the White House. Alberto Gonzales rose to the very top of his profession when the president appointed him attorney general of the United States. This made him the top law enforcement officer of the land, holding the same lofty office that Robert Kennedy had held under his brother, President John F. Kennedy.

All this from a humble man from a humble home who applies the principle of going the extra mile every day. In every way.

Only the Smart Few Get It

Going the extra mile, in my opinion, is one of the easiest principles to apply. And it works like magic! All you have to do is do more than you are paid to do. Do it every day. Do it with a positive mental attitude. It is the principle that gets the most return in the least time. I say this because I've seen it work time and time again.

One of the most memorable examples of going the extra mile is that of Antonio Rivera, a small, friendly man with a thin mustache and slicked-back thin gray hair who lived in the Rio Grande Valley in Texas. Tony was a furniture salesman. You know, one of those fellas who dashes out to greet you whenever you walk into a furniture store to look around. *"¿En que le puedo servir?"* is usually their first question. "How may I serve you?"

He started out as many young salesmen do, by taking a job in a local store to sell what he could. He was one of five salespeople in a family-owned furniture store. When a new customer walked in the door, a different salesperson would take a turn to make the next sale. Each turn was called an "up."

"I'm up!"

"No, I'm up!"

"You were out for a smoke. You lost your up!"

"*Pinche vato,* cheater!"

Sometimes there were big fights right in front of the customer as the alpha dogs worked it out. The first few years as Tony was learning the ropes, he was one of those dogs. As he learned the ropes he got smarter. Instead of trying to make a quick sale and hurry to get back in line for the next up, he tried a new angle. Going the extra mile. He took extra time to serve the customer. As much time as they wanted. He accompanied them through the store as they shopped, giving decorating suggestions and advice along the way.

They didn't always buy at first. But when they returned, they asked for Tony. The rule was, when a customer asked for any specific salesperson, it didn't matter whose up it was, the request was accommodated. Little by little, more people began asking for him. Many times he stayed after hours serving customers. He enjoyed it. Even when the sale turned out to be only a small lamp. Tony noticed that the more quality time he spent with his customers, the bigger his commission checks were. But he didn't stop there when he became top salesman. Instead, he began thinking of ways to improve even more.

¿Qué más puedo hacer? "What more could I do?" he asked himself. Then he got another idea. He began to keep a file of every item each customer bought. He even offered to visit customers' homes to make sure that the sofa, chair, or carpet they were buying would fit properly and comfortably in their home. He drew diagrams of each room to have a more complete record. He watched carefully as new items came in the store, keeping his customers in mind. If he thought a certain item and price was right for a certain person, he called them and gave them "first dibs" at the new merchandise.

"A new chair just came in that is perfect for your bedroom. It's the style you like. The color will complement your drapes. And the price is a steal. Do you want to come see it, or should I take it to you in my pickup so you can see it in your room?"

"You'll do that for me?"

"*Seguro que sí.* You are my client. I want to give you first shot at this. I think you will love it!"

He Didn't Stop There

By then, Tony didn't even worry about who was "up" at the front of the store. He was at the back of the store, calling clients, and unpacking crates to see what new pieces he could find, and whose home it would fit in best. Each day he made dozens of calls. He also visited two or three homes a day making new diagrams and updating his files. Every time a new store sale was about to take place, he would call his favorite clients with news of the best deals.

The other salespeople were impressed at Tony's salesmanship and rising income. They saw him going the extra mile every day. They saw him making the extra calls and staying late, all with a big smile on his face. They even got to see and examine Tony's growing files, which now filled a dozen three-ring binders. When they asked Tony how he did it, he told them. He demonstrated exactly how they could do the same thing. He went so far with the idea of the extra mile, he even gave his "secrets" away.

Guess what? No one copied him. Perhaps they thought it would be too much work. Maybe they felt it simply was not required of them. I believe that their force of habit was stronger than their desire for success. So they went back to doing what they had been doing all along—sitting nervously at the front of the store, drinking coffee, and waiting for their next up while Tony was raking in 60 percent of the store sales. The others never saw his paychecks. If they had, perhaps they too would have given Tony's techniques a try. But then again, maybe not. Only 2 percent of the population applies all seventeen principles of personal achievement to reach their major definite purpose. Are you in the top 2 percent?

When Tony retired a couple of years ago, he made a gift of his notebooks to the remaining sales team. I haven't visited the store lately, but I often wonder if a new Tony has gotten hold of them.

7

Personal Initiative —Raul Romero

"There are two types of individuals who never amount to anything," Andrew Carnegie once told Napoleon Hill. "Those who never do anything except what they're told to do. And those who cannot do (or will not do) what they're supposed to do."

We all know people who try to get ahead without much effort. They don't go far. Those who achieve success understand that to get something worthwhile, *you must do something worthwhile.* Successful people have a habit of going the extra mile. They don't expect an opportunity to fall in their lap. *They have the personal initiative to go out and make it happen.*

Personal Initiative Succeeds Where Others Fail

During the 2000 presidential race, George W. Bush decided that Latinos should do his official welcoming at the Republican National Convention in Philadelphia. This was something no candidate of either party had ever thought of before. "We'll make the first event of the week a giant Latino event. A big salsa party to kick off the convention," he told the planners.

They called a meeting. My wife Kathy and I were there to help design the graphics, come up with a theme for the event, and produce a video.

Everyone there had big ideas of what to do. "Let's get the biggest stars we can find!" one volunteer offered.

"Excellent thought," said another. "How about Ricky Martin, Gloria Estefan, Emilio Estefan, and Celia Cruz?"

"Perfect, we should have two big salsa bands and get Jon Secada to sing a bilingual version of the song *America!*"

"Somebody needs to find a place to hold it."

"How about the art museum, where Rocky ran up the steps in the movie?"

Beth Sturgeon, the person in charge of fund-raising, was crunching numbers. "Looks like this party will cost a million dollars! And that's assuming somebody here can get all these big-name performers to donate their time. Security alone will cost a fortune. Where's the money coming from?"

"Isn't it in the budget?" I asked.

"No, we have to raise it. And we've got seven weeks!"

Right about that time, all eyes turned toward the center of the table. There sat Raul Romero, a bubbly yet suave, distinguished-looking man in his forties with a perpetual smile on his face. Everyone knew him. They also knew his reputation. Raul had been George W. Bush's first Latino *Pioneer,* someone who'd raised a hundred thousand dollars for Bush's campaign.

"We can do it," he said with a big smile on his face. "I'll raise the million. You guys make it happen." Planning was one thing. Raising a million dollars in seven weeks was another. But if anyone could do it, it was Raul. Before the meeting ended, we each got our assignments and went to work.

When we came back to report a month later, Raul's smile was

bigger than usual. "Ladies and gentlemen," he said, "we have one million, seven hundred thousand dollars in our piggy bank. Let's throw a party!"

And what a party it was! The two bands and all the stars were there. Choirs of small children sang the bilingual version of *America* along with Jon Secada. The museum plaza was covered wall to wall with enthusiastic Latinos and citizens of Philly. When George W. Bush walked in, the worldwide press was there to send the message the world over.

History was made that day. Never before in American politics had a presidential candidate been welcomed to a national convention by his Latino supporters. Raul was in the crowd watching as the festivities unfolded. His beaming smile reflected the significance of the historic moment. None of this would have ever happened without Romero's deft hand. It was an impressive feat. What is even more impressive is that he didn't stop when he reached the one million dollar mark. He just kept going. He was on a roll. The contributors he called on wanted in. They were happy to get out their checkbooks and sign up. All because of Raul Romero's personal initiative.

Raul does things like this all the time. He never waits to be told what to do. He raised the first hundred thousand dollars for George W. Bush because he wanted to help him become president of the United States. He raised the next $1.7 million because he saw the opportunity for the future president to make history. Personal initiative is what Raul Romero is all about.

Personal Initiative Is Contagious

The moment Raul declared, "I'll raise the million, you make it happen," everyone in the room was committed, too. No one could dare say, "I can't do my part, it's too hard." Raul had us and we all knew it. We also knew he wouldn't let us down. So we couldn't let each other down. Much less George W. Bush.

The full team was put in place. Warren Tichenor was the celebrity talent guru as well as the "go-to" man behind Hispanic Republican politics. He'd been the dean of Spanish radio in America and had the cell phone number of every Latino personality and celebrity in the world. He could get the big names to the party. On time and on budget.

Leonard Rodriguez and Brent Gilmore took care of security, tickets, signage, and getting the crowd. Ronnie Arredondo designed the graphics. Cesar Martinez saw to it that all the banners, graphics, and videos were produced and in place. Abel Guerra made sure everyone knew his or her drill and got to the party on time. Jennifer Bogart had the savvy to coordinate the entire event. It came off perfectly.

Raul's personal initiative is contagious. It invigorates people and makes believers of everyone. It makes the impossible happen. Without him, this special and historic welcome for the president-to-be would not have happened. After all, without a million bucks, you can't have a million-dollar event.

Personal Initiative Creates Advancement

What characteristic creates personal initiative in an individual? Why do some people have it and others don't? Are we born with it? Can we learn it? Can we have it and lose it? Can one cultivate it if it's not present? These are intriguing questions.

Lack of personal initiative and laziness are closely related. People who are lazy or who lack personal initiative are happy with the way things are. If you are happy with poverty, you will not generate the personal initiative to do the hard work necessary to make you rich. If music isn't your thing, you will lack the personal initiative to put in the long hours of practice it takes to learn to play an instrument well.

Perhaps you know a teenager who lacks personal initiative. They sleep until noon on weekends and are slow to do their chores, even when reminded. They love to party, visit friends, borrow the family car, and stay up all hours watching TV, even on school nights. Why do they lack the personal initiative to change for the better? Because they like it the way it is! All they have to do is put up with some serious nagging. Why would they want to change? They have the perfect place to eat, sleep, watch TV, and "chill." Things couldn't be better. In this case, there would be no reason to want to change. No personal initiative is needed.

That same teen, a few years later, may be different altogether. Let's say he's out on his own, not earning much, with no pocket cash, no car, living in a cramped apartment with two messy roommates, and eating pizza leftovers most nights. He may decide he doesn't like this situation. Only he can make the decision to change things. To do that, he will have to exercise the personal initiative to go out and secure a job that pays well enough to make things more like they were when he lived with his parents.

Personal initiative is present in all of us. *It is nothing more than the exercising of the free will we were gifted with at birth.* We can use it any place we like. We can use it any time we like. Personal initiative can change anything from a bad habit to the course your life takes. All you have to do is decide to use it.

Personal Initiative Creates the Future

Raul Romero's parents and grandparents were big influences in his life. They were committed to education and to its value to Raul's future. They actually sold the family home in Panama to raise the tuition and expense money to send Raul to college. They had a plan for him. That plan fueled the personal initiative it took to sacrifice their property. They knew it would pay off.

Raulito had been a great student in Panama—consistently ranking first in his class. His parents encouraged him to attend Cambridge University in England, where he had qualified. At the time, college antiwar demonstrations were being held often in the United States. "What if Raul starts acting like those *gringitos* and becomes a hippie?" they asked.

It didn't happen. An uncle living in the United States had a son enrolled at the University of Notre Dame. "Don't worry, send Raul to me. He'll do great here and I'll make sure he behaves," he promised.

"Notre Dame changed my life," Raul explains. "The place rooted me. I learned a profession. Even more important, I learned values. The university strengthened my desire to be the best. I learned that after you climb one mountain, you usually look for a higher one to climb."

He pauses, smiles, and adds, "I don't wait for opportunity. I go out and find it. Then I go for it. There are no traffic jams on the highway of the extra mile." Napoleon Hill couldn't have said it any better.

The Major Attributes of Personal Achievement

In the years Napoleon Hill spent formulating these principles of success, he observed many extraordinary people. What follows is a list of the qualities that constantly appeared in his observations. Some of them have already been covered in this book—others come later. The important thing for you to do here, he says, is to identify these characteristics in yourself. And then to think about how you can increase and strengthen them.

1. Having a definite major purpose
2. Being motivated to pursue that purpose continually
3. A mastermind alliance through which to achieve the purpose
4. Self-reliance
5. Self-discipline
6. Persistence, based on the will to win
7. Well-developed imagination, controlled and directed
8. A habit of prompt, definite decision making
9. A habit of basing opinions on known facts, not guesswork
10. A habit of going the extra mile
11. A capacity to control enthusiasm
12. A well-developed sense of details
13. The capacity to listen to criticism without resentment
14. Familiarity with the ten basic human motives
15. The capacity to direct attention to one task at a time
16. Willingness to assume full responsibility for one's own actions
17. Willingness to accept responsibility for the mistakes of subordinates
18. Patience with subordinates and associates
19. Recognizing the merits and abilities of others
20. A positive mental attitude at all times
21. A capacity for applied faith
22. A habit of following through
23. A habit of emphasizing thoroughness instead of speed
24. Dependability

When I look at this list, written so long ago, I marvel at how timeless it is. And when I compare the list to the qualities Raul demonstrates on a daily basis, I marvel at the fact that they are one and the same.

President Bush didn't limit Raul's talents to the campaign. He wanted him to serve in his administration and asked, "What do you want to do?" At this point, Raul could have asked to be appointed to any number of plum jobs in government. Instead, he said, "Mr. President, I'd like to spend the next eight years finding the most talented Hispanics to serve in your administration."

The president agreed. Raul went to work with his usual zeal. Through his efforts, more Latinos now serve in government and in the White House than ever before. Raul Romero has already left a legacy that will not be soon forgotten. And he's just getting started.

8

Positive Mental Attitude
—Linda Alvarado

People who have a positive mental attitude can overcome great obstacles. As an example, let's take a person we all know—Bill Clinton. As president, he didn't let scandal get him down. When the Monica Lewinsky issue was in full swing, he stayed focused on his work. He looked confident and upbeat despite the turmoil. In fact, he delivered one of the best State of the Union addresses of his presidency while the news of his impending impeachment dominated the world's front pages.

Richard Nixon, on the other hand, was not a positive person. His presidency ended with his resignation, largely because he let negativity and distrust of people permeate his core, leading to the Watergate scandal. Clinton survived impeachment, and Nixon quit to avoid it. The difference? A positive mental attitude.

How a Positive Mental Attitude Develops

A positive mental attitude is the most important principle in the science of success, Napoleon Hill says. I couldn't agree more. This amazing principle worked for me the moment I learned to apply it at the age of twenty-three. I had just graduated from the Napoleon Hill School of Personal Achievement—the course that taught the same seventeen principles of personal achievement you are reading about now. The idea of developing and keeping a positive mental attitude had been drilled into each student's brain every week for seventeen weeks. Now it was time to put this learning to the test.

I began by opening up my own part-time business, a graphic art studio. My initial plan was to make eight sales calls every day during a two-week vacation at the sign shop where I was working. I called on some of the best and biggest ad agencies and print shops in San Antonio, selling myself as the best, fastest, and cheapest graphic designer in town.

Jim Anderson, then manager of Aylin Advertising, responded. He gave me my first big break with an assignment and a challenge: "Do the finished artwork for these three magazine ads," he said. "Bring back the completed work in two days along with your invoice. Let's see what you can do."

Wow! "I'm in business!" I thought. Immediately I went home and completed the task doing the best job I could as fast as I could.

The next day, beating the deadline by twenty-four hours, I delivered the three completed ads to Jim's office with an invoice for twenty-seven dollars. It read, "Three ads at nine dollars each, twenty-seven dollars total." The whole job had taken me no more than nine hours to complete. In figuring out what to charge, I had made some calculations. At my regular job at Texas Neon, I was earning a dollar ten an hour. Keeping a positive mental attitude, I decided to charge three dollars an hour for my work. I was a little unsure about it, but what the heck? All he could say was "no way."

When I handed him the artwork, Jim took a look at it. "Good job," he said. Then he looked at my invoice. "Twenty-seven dollars? No way!"

Oops! Had my positive mental attitude gotten me in trouble? Had I misused it?

"Listen, Lionel," Jim whispered. "You need to charge more than this. Your work is worth at least a hundred dollars. Besides, I earn my money by marking up my suppliers' invoices 15 percent. I should earn fifteen dollars on your bill instead of a measly five and change. Make me a new invoice, okay?"

My mouth hung open. I had just earned a hundred dollars for a day's work! That was twice as much as I earned in a whole week at the sign shop! The feeling of excitement and newfound self-worth was awesome. Up until that time, I hadn't experienced this feeling. It made me a believer in the power of a positive mental attitude. It gave me self-confidence. It taught me to think big.

The Choice Is Yours to Make

A positive mental attitude will bring a multitude of good things to your life. By making it a lifelong habit, you can pretty much choose the type of future you want to have. If you choose to develop a positive mental attitude, you will begin to enjoy a "success consciousness" that will give you good health, both mentally and physically. It will give you financial independence and peace of mind. It will replace fear with faith and confidence. It will help you nurture enduring friendships and will tear down the barriers of self-imposed limitations. It will give you the wisdom to understand yourself and others.

Many people choose not to learn to develop a positive mental attitude. They choose not to exercise the self-discipline required to make it part of their lives. People with negative mental attitudes are doomed to a life of misery. They suffer mental and physical ailments of all kinds. They are held back by self-imposed limitations. They get trapped in mediocrity. They become fearful and worry needlessly. They become the victims of every negative influence they encounter. In short, they waste their entire lives and do little to improve the human condition.

"It's up to you to make the choice," Napoleon Hill says. "By not choosing to develop a positive mental attitude, you are choosing to misuse your true potential. There is no halfway point," he says, "no compromise."

What choice will you make?

The Rewards of a Positive Mental Attitude

As Latinos, many of us wrestle with the concept of *consciously* learning to develop and sustain a positive mental attitude. To many of us, it just doesn't seem natural. So we question it. "What if developing a positive mental attitude results in riches I don't deserve? What if my newfound success is more than I can handle? What if my family and friends accuse me of selling out? Doesn't this whole idea suggest that I would be *imposing* my own will over that of my Creator?"

Good questions. As a young man, I had them, too. It took me years of research in my career in marketing to discover why.

As you learned in the foreword to this book, Latino core values are based on Catholicism, the Spanish conquest, and respect for the status quo. We are expected to be humble, respectful, and polite. Many of us are taught that wealthy people are unhappy, mean, and miserly. Others of us grow up thinking that if we stay poor, we are more likely to go to heaven. Latino society in the Americas developed as a class society that separated the poorer indigenous Indian population from that of their conquerors, the upper-class

Spaniard. It was them and us. The Spaniards were the rich and light-skinned *rubios*. The Indians were the dark and poor *inditos*. I'm exaggerating to make the point, but you get the idea.

In the media, we get all kinds of positive attitude messages. "Just do it! Be all that you can be. Have it your way." As Latinos, we are attracted to these messages even though they are based on a set of values different from our own. They are based on the Puritan, Protestant, and Calvinistic teachings of the Anglo: hard work, success, and wealth based on individual ability and desire. Both these sets of values have a lot going for them. We can learn to take a little from one and a little from the other to make it work for us. This book will teach you how.

Combining the Values of the Cultures for Success

Most successful Latinos and Latinas run their lives by combining Anglo and Latino values. They pick. They choose. They keep the parts having to do with family, hard work, and personal responsibility. They lose the parts that promote the idea of staying too poor, behaving too humbly, and "not rocking the boat."

Linda Alvarado is one of them. She is president and CEO of Alvarado Construction. Her firm is one of the biggest construction contractors in the country. It is the biggest headed by a woman. Alvarado Construction has helped build the Colorado Convention Center, the Denver International Airport, and the new stadium for the Denver Broncos. Linda shattered the glass ceiling in both the private business and corporate worlds. She was a member of the board of directors of Norwest Bank while still in her twenties. Within a few years she became a director of several Fortune 500 companies, including Qwest Communications, the Pepsi Bottling Group, 3M, Pitney Bowes, and Lenox International. At thirty-nine, Linda made history by becoming the youngest woman to be a part-owner of a major-league baseball team, the Colorado Rockies.

Given this great success at such an early age, one might think that this woman might have inherited the construction company from her father. Maybe she had been born with a silver spoon in her mouth. Not so. Linda was one of six children and the only girl in a family of very modest means. There was no running water in the house. By government standards, the family was living in poverty. By their standards, they were living the American Dream. In the land of opportunity.

The Martinezes were Baptist. Linda's father was a proud man with Spanish roots, a quick mind, and a positive mental attitude. *"No tenemos mucho,"* he would say. *"Pero tenemos más que muchos."* He believed it. "We may not have much. But we have more than many."

At Christmas and at Thanksgiving, Linda's dad would round up the family so that they could take food to the less fortunate. Helping the needy was taken seriously at the Martinez household. "Caring for others is a demonstration of your own self-worth," he would say. His wife agreed, adding, "Money is not the measure of who you are. How you serve others is."

The 2 Percent Who Succeed

Most people don't realize the difference between wishing and believing, says Napoleon Hill. This is because so many folks *mistake a wish for a goal.* They *wish* they could start a business. They *wish* they could play the piano. They *wish* they could go back to school. They don't know it takes six steps to help them use their minds to attain their desires. Here's a list of those steps:

1. First you *wish* for success.
2. Then you *desire* it.
3. Now you *hope* you'll achieve it.
4. Then you start *believing* you can.

5. Next you *expect* success.

6. Finally you *achieve* it.

Most people go through life only *wishing* for success and doing nothing else.

Ten percent turn their wishes into real *desires*. They think about what they want constantly but do nothing more.

Eight percent take it to the next step. They turn their wishes and desires into *hopes*.

Six percent of the population translates hope into the real *belief* that what they want will actually happen.

Four percent of people crystallize their wishes into the *expectation* that their goal will become real.

Only 2 percent take the final step toward the *achievement* of their goal.

Are you one of the 2 percent? Most probably. The fact that you've gotten this far in the book is proof.

One of the Boys

Linda Alvarado is definitely in the top 2 percent of the U.S. population in terms of achieving success. As far as she was concerned, growing up as the only girl in a family with five brothers had more advantages than disadvantages. First, as you might guess, it taught her to share. It taught her to be competitive. To be athletic. To understand the power of negotiating with men. She also gained valuable insights into the nuances of the male psyche, including one-upmanship and "Guy Humor." Learning the way men trade jabs and make jokes at the other's expense was key. This inside knowledge prepared her for the competitive male-oriented business in which she was to prosper.

Surviving in the nearly all-male household developed young Linda's self-esteem. It heightened her competitive spirit. And because her brothers were always expecting to beat her at most any-thing, she worked harder to beat them. When she topped them in sports or in school, it gave her even more confidence. "I can do more than others expect," she thought to herself.

Mr. and Mrs. Martinez encouraged their children's natural sib-ling rivalry, especially in sports. They saw it as an opportunity to teach the children that it was better to win, not by excluding, but by including. They taught the kids to play by the rules—to move from one position to another as they played but to always stay in the game. The Martinez clan also learned to brush off blame and guilt when it came to dropping a ball or losing a game.

The brothers considered Linda "one of the boys." The ques-tion was, would she get this same respect from the guys in the work-place? You can guess the answer.

No.

Not too surprising considering that Linda had decided to make construction, the paramount macho man's domain, her career. "What are you trying to prove?" they asked.

"I can build anything, I've built forts in my backyard," she replied.

"Well then, stay and play in your backyard, little girl," was the curt and demeaning reply.

Linda didn't go back. She wanted to play. The way she always had—with the boys.

A Positive Mental Attitude Turns Nos to Yeses

Every day, Linda scoured the newspapers in search of opportunities for a job in construction. When she was offered part-time jobs mowing lawns and helping landscape new homes, she declined. Only a real construction position would do. She got a lot of nos as she filled out countless applications and went on dozens of inter-views.

"What are you doing here?"

"I'm here for the position," she announced on one particular interview.

"But you're a girl."

"I can do the job. Besides, I'm looking at your ad. Where does it say, 'boys only'?"

"Okay, we're an equal opportunity employer. We'll give you a chance."

Linda was hired, albeit reluctantly. The foreman was convinced that he could make her miserable enough to quit. He gave her the toughest jobs. The dirtiest assignments. The nastiest supervisors. Still, she hung in there, fueled by her positive mental attitude. And her main definite purpose.

In the evenings Linda took classes in surveying, scheduling, and estimating. While at the local community college, she got the idea to go into business for herself. She was in her early twenties and had no money. No credit. No collateral. No contacts. No contracts. But she had an idea. First, she hung out her shingle: L.G. Alvarado, Alvarado Construction Inc. Then she began calling on the big general contractors to convince them to let her do small jobs building street curbs for their new developments.

"There's no risk for you," she smiled on one interview. "I'll even let you pay the concrete company directly, saving you my usual 20 percent mark-up. You'll make a better profit and I'll get an opportunity to show what I can do. It's a win-win situation. Just take a look at my bid."

Linda's price was so reasonable that the contractor couldn't refuse it. He accepted her bid and Alvarado Construction was in business! What the fellow didn't know was that Linda couldn't have paid for the concrete in the first place: She had no credit. In an interesting and creative way, the contractor helped to finance Alvarado Construction. It couldn't have worked out better.

Building concrete curbs became Linda's bread and butter. She went after every contract she could find, but the bigger jobs still eluded her. To get them, she would have to raise the capital needed to hire people and buy materials to be able to bid for the big contracts. Her parents came to the rescue. They had been watching her work. It was clear to them that their daughter was serious. So they mortgaged their home at a high interest rate and loaned her twenty-five hundred dollars. The company started to grow by landing the contract to build bus shelters all over town. Amazingly, the relatively inexperienced Latina was attracting and hiring some of the best journeymen in the area. They liked Linda's positive familial culture and were inspired by her desire to be the best.

She was a girl, so what? She was young, no matter. Linda proved every day that she could work as hard as any man. And lead as well as any.

"You can see how a positive mental attitude relies upon and reinforces so many of the principles crucial to personal achievement," Napoleon Hill says. In Linda Alvarado, you can see it clearly.

9

Controlled Enthusiasm —Sara Martinez Tucker

Enthusiasm is the fuel that drives you forward toward your definite major purpose. Napoleon Hill likens it to gasoline. Properly used, it will get you to your destination. But watch out! Improperly or prematurely ignited, the outcome can be disastrous. Your definite purpose could go up in flames.

I meet enthusiastic people all the time. The successful ones direct their enthusiasm in a very deliberate way. It is not always overt but it can always be felt. They seem to have a knack for using their gasoline efficiently. Unsuccessful individuals tend to grab an idea, many times the first one they get, and move forward with it. They assume it's a great idea just because it's theirs, and don't give much thought to the barriers and opportunities before them. Other people can ruin a good idea or a good cause with overzealousness.

The Dangers of Uncontrolled Enthusiasm

Enthusiasm without forethought happens all the time. It happened in epidemic proportions in the late 1990s during the dot-com craze. Greed drove unbridled enthusiasm to make a buck like never before. The gasoline of enthusiasm spilled over like an overturned eighteen-wheeler and set the stock market ablaze. When the fire burned itself out, millions of investors had lost billions of dollars. Entire fortunes were wiped out. Billionaires became paupers and small day traders lost their life savings.

Some very smart people got caught up in the ballyhoo, assuming that the Internet was the future—a new category of business they didn't quite understand. As it turned out, the Internet is a way of doing business, not a business unto itself.

The Benefits of Controlled Enthusiasm

Not everyone was fooled. Warren Buffett, America's preeminent investor, never took the bait. He never quite understood the merit of investing in companies that didn't have a plan to make a profit. He was right. Most others were wrong. Buffett refused to let his enthusiasm for investing in the stock market lead him astray. He kept doing what he'd always done: investing in companies with potential and sound business practices. He not only kept his fortune, he increased it.

Ted Turner, the creator of CNN, is a man who gets very enthusiastic about everything he undertakes. He succeeds because he makes good assumptions based on accurate observation. Some twenty years ago, he assumed the world needed a twenty-four hour television news network *because he needed it*. Turner wished he could catch the evening news at whatever time he came home from his day's work. Because he usually worked late, the 6 p.m. television network news was over.

He figured he wasn't the only person in the world who needed to access television news at midnight or any other time. He was right. CNN was an idea whose time had come. It became a reality as a result of his enthusiasm for the idea. This deliberate enthusiasm fueled his major purpose and forever changed the way most of the world gets its news on television.

How to Develop Controlled Enthusiasm

Sara Martinez Tucker is the president of the Hispanic Scholarship Fund (HSF). She exemplifies controlled enthusiasm better than anyone I know. She is a woman on a mission. Her definite major purpose is to help strengthen America by elevating Latino educational opportunities.

The first time I saw her make a presentation on behalf of HSF, I was taken by her poise, command of the subject matter, and communication skills. I'm in the advertising business, so I've seen hundreds of first-class presentations made at the highest levels of business and government. None are as good as Sara's.

When she walks into a room, she's calm, friendly, confident, and exquisitely attired. Her enthusiasm is under perfect control. She knows the names of the people attending. She knows their business backgrounds, and often something about them personally. She knows exactly what she wants out of the meeting and states it up front. She speaks in a clear voice, keeping the group engaged with relevant stories and pertinent information. She doesn't use notes. Her facts and figures are accurate, complete, and committed to memory. She reads body language skillfully, and tactfully converts each person to the HSF cause. By the time the presentation is over, strangers have become friends and the sale has been made.

Under her leadership, the Hispanic Scholarship Fund has grown from three million dollars in scholarship awards per year to over one hundred million over the past four. She took a small, struggling organization and, with the help of her mastermind alliance and a top-notch team, grew it to one of the largest and most respected Latino organizations in the nation. President George W. Bush and the heads of some of America's leading foundations and Fortune 500 corporations have praised her work publicly. I credit her success to her amazing controlled enthusiasm.

Sara began to develop this talent as a young girl in the deep southern Texas town of Laredo. Laredo's population is 95 percent Mexican. Latinos there don't much feel like a minority because they aren't—and never have been. There is a confident, breezy, and enthusiastic character to Laredoans. They go about the business of living and succeeding unencumbered by the prejudices of the outside world.

In grade school and throughout high school, Sara was a hard worker, yet quiet and shy. Her dad worked for the Texas Employment Commission and her mom for the local bank. To augment the family income, her parents bought a small convenience store near downtown when Sara was nine and her brother, Neto, was seven. Both the kids were put to work at the store as soon as it opened for business. They worked after school and all day during the summers, alternating their hours and days to make time for their homework and household chores. At the store, Sara first learned to translate effort into income. The harder and smarter she worked, the more she could earn. She got enthusiastic about that. She got even more excited about the world outside Laredo, Texas.

"This is not enough," she thought. "There must be something better out there."

Both her mom and her dad encouraged this thinking. "We have no connections in Laredo and little exposure to the outside world," they advised. " There are bigger things out there for you, *hija*. Go to the big city, meet people, and do big things."

The big city was Austin, and the big place to meet people and to do big things was the University of Texas with its fifty thousand students. Having been valedictorian of her high school graduating class, Sara's admission was automatic. There she was, enrolled in one of the best public universities in the nation. She was about to understand what her mother had meant when she warned her about having had "little exposure."

On her first day in English literature, the class was given the reading list for the semester. She overheard a group of students: "This is going to be easy! We read this stuff in the ninth grade!" Sara realized that *she'd never even heard* of any of those books. "In Laredo, I was the pick of the litter," she said to herself. "In Austin I'm the runt."

Sara now knew she would have to make up for lost time. Her fantasy of "something different from Laredo" had come true, and it was time to go to work. In college, everything mattered to Sara. She became aware of the value of every hour. Of every minute. Of every penny. Her budget for lunch each day was ninety-seven cents. By the time she graduated with honors at Texas, she had learned the first of three phases of controlled enthusiasm. *She had talent—she could do it!*

Right out of college, the hard-charging journalism major was hired on by the *San Antonio Express-News* as the "Action Express" reporter, assigned to identify and help solve community problems. She tackled the job with the same enthusiastic drive. She never left her office until her in-box was empty. She was happy, but soon began to feel that force tugging at her again. "I need to get myself out of South Texas. There must be something better out there."

After earning her MBA, she still wasn't sure what that "something better" would be. She was about to find out. Her next adventure was New York and a big corporation, AT&T. Now on a business track, she moved up the ladder quickly. Soon she was a vice president and the highest-ranking Hispanic female executive, the only Hispanic female officer among AT&T's thirty-three thousand employees.

At AT&T, she learned to be a business leader—to write a business plan, to speak up and be heard. She also perfected the discipline of preparation. "In God we trust," her boss said, "all others bring data." The second lesson in the three phases of controlled enthusiasm kicked in: *She had a voice—she could use it!*

Sara was then asked to serve on the board of directors of the Hispanic Scholarship Fund. AT&T was thinking of making a bigger investment in the fund and assigned Sara to assess the potential of the organization. Serving as a volunteer there, it became apparent to her that the "something better" was unfolding before her eyes.

Sara began to see how much the Hispanic Scholarship Fund meant to the future of young Latinos in America. The more she learned, the more she wanted to be a bigger part of it. When Ernest Robles, the fund's founding president, retired, Sara was offered the position. She took it. It felt so right. This was the place for her. The third lesson in controlled enthusiasm rounded out her learning. *You've got a heart—show it!*

Enthusiasm Changes Lives

Sara exhibited controlled enthusiasm in each of her three careers. As a student, journalist, and reporter, she learned her talent for communicating effectively and used it. As a top executive in a Fortune 500 company, she discovered her talent for business and accountability. Finally, as president of the Hispanic Scholarship Fund, she has found her heart. And her calling. Enthusiasm drove her forward toward her definite major purpose. Napoleon Hill would be proud of her. Controlled enthusiasm got her to her rightful destination. She had the discipline to see to it that her fuel never spilled over.

How to Develop Controlled Enthusiasm

A final thought on this chapter. Follow Napoleon Hill's eleven rules of controlled enthusiasm and you too will achieve your major purpose in life. Here they are, exactly as he wrote them:

1. Adopt a definite major purpose.
2. Write out a clear statement of that purpose and your plan for attaining it. Include a statement of what you intend to give in return for its realization.
3. Back your purpose with a burning desire. Fan that desire, coax it; let it become the dominating thought in your mind.
4. Set to work immediately in carrying out your plan.
5. Follow your plan accurately and persistently.
6. If you are overtaken by defeat, study your plan carefully and change it if necessary. Do not change it simply because you have met defeat.
7. Ally yourself with others whose help you need.
8. Keep away from joy-killers and nay-sayers. Stick with the optimists.
9. *Never let a day pass without devoting some time to furthering your plan.* You are developing enthusiasm as a habit, and habits require reinforcement.
10. Keep yourself sold on the idea that you will attain your definite major purpose, no matter how far away that moment seems. Autosuggestion is a powerful force in the development of enthusiasm.
11. Keep your mind positive at all times. Enthusiasm will not thrive in an environment of fear, envy, greed, jealousy, doubt, revenge, hatred, intolerance, and procrastination. It needs positive thought and action.

10

Self-Discipline
—Patricia Diaz Dennis

Self-discipline is the funnel through which the other important principles of personal achievement flow. Without self-discipline, even the loftiest of dreams will eventually dissipate. Without self-discipline, your main definite purpose will become a meaningless wild-goose chase. Your pleasing personality will get you nowhere. Your boundless enthusiasm will spew and flail about uncontrollably like an unheld water hose at full pressure. Even applied faith will not give you the rudder you need to steer your ship steadily ahead. Only by applying self-discipline will you produce the positive results you want in life.

Napoleon Hill teaches that your mind is much like a reservoir that stores up potential power. If you think of it as such, you will learn to release this power in precise increments, at specific times, and following exact trajectories. This, he says, is the essence of controlled attention.

Controlling Your Emotions

That Latinos are emotional people may be a stereotype. Surely we're not the only people who sometimes act first and think about the consequences only later. Latino or not, people get in trouble when they let emotional rewards control their actions. Immediate gratification is an emotional reward. Spending money gives some people so much gratification that it gives them the "permission" to spend more than they earn. These people can ruin their credit, lose their assets, or even lose their home. The pleasure of watching television can turn a healthy, athletic person into an overweight couch potato.

Enforcing self-discipline will reverse the process of acting before thinking, Hill said: *"It will instill in you the habit of thinking before acting."*

To control our emotions, we must first understand them. Napoleon Hill studied the positive and negative emotions we all experience. He identified the positive emotions:

1. *amor,* "love"
2. *sexo,* "sex"
3. *esperanza,* "hope"
4. *fe,* "faith"
5. *entusiasmo,* "enthusiasm"
6. *lealtad,* "loyalty"
7. *deseo,* "desire"

Study these words. First in Spanish, then in English. Notice how the language seems to change the meaning of words? Do the words *sexo* and *deseo* ring as positively in Spanish as they do in English? They don't, do they? Remember this: The meaning words have in one language may not be *exactly* the same in another. These subtle differences can and will affect the way we Latinos interpret the words and concepts of the Anglo world.

Hill identifies negative emotions also:

1. *miedo,* "fear"
2. *celo,* "jealousy"
3. *odio,* "hatred"
4. *venganza,* "revenge"
5. *codicia,* "greed"
6. *enojo,* "anger"
7. *superstición,* "superstition"

Here again, language affects the way we interpret certain words. Many Latinos mistake the word *ambicioso,* "ambitious," for "greedy." In the United States, ambition is good. In Mexico and many parts of Latin America, ambition is often perceived as greed. Why? Perhaps when the conquistador taught the *indígeno* the Spanish language, he changed the meaning just enough to make ambition something of a negative. After all, it would be a lot harder to conquer people with ambition.

All emotions, positive and negative, are strong. Strong enough to control you if you don't control them. You have the power to control negative emotions to keep them from steering you off course. You also have the power to capitalize on positive emotions to keep you on the road to success.

Control Emotions with Self-Discipline

For several years, I have watched Patricia Diaz Dennis practice self-discipline consistently. So consistently, in fact, that she has attained most every goal she has ever set for herself.

In early 2005, she was elected chair of the Girl Scouts of the USA—the first Latina to ever serve in this national leadership role. She has been a trailblazer most everywhere she's been. She was the first Latina to serve as a U.S. federal communications commissioner, the first Latina to serve on the National Labor Relations Board, and the first to serve as an assistant secretary of state for human rights. All of these are presidential appointments. Patricia was also the first Hispanic woman to attain the level of senior vice president, general counsel, and corporate secretary to SBC Communication's Pacific Bell and Nevada Bell. Her resume of achievements is so long it could fill this whole chapter. It is so inspiring that it *will* fill this chapter.

Her success in life and ability to apply self-discipline began with the words her father often repeated as she was growing up. "*Eres inteligente y bonita,* you are smart and pretty," he would say. Being a child, Patricia took her father's words as fact. She assumed she was smart and pretty. That assumption (which happens to be correct) had a strong effect on Patricia for the first fourteen years of her life. On the one hand, it gave her great confidence. She became a popular cheerleader, made good grades, and was elected class president. On the other hand, it gave her *so* much confidence that she assumed that she wouldn't have to work very hard to get ahead. She also assumed that she could ignore the things that didn't come easy to her. Like math.

Life was grand. The family was living in exotic places like Japan and Chile where her father, a sergeant in the Army, was stationed. This travel was good for her. It gave her a sense of the world outside her home state of New Mexico.

Things changed dramatically for Patricia in the ninth grade. Her teacher, Mrs. Winifred Smith, noticed that in spite of her good grades, she wasn't working to her full potential. "You can do better," she said. "Don't settle for being mediocre."

The Power of Self-Discipline

Those words fell like a ton of bricks on Patricia. They made a life-long impression. "I didn't want to be mediocre. I didn't even want to be *thought of* as mediocre," she recalls. "I want to be recognized for being the best at what I do. I care about what people think of me and, more importantly, what I think of myself. So I started to put a lot more effort into everything. Especially toward the things I *didn't* like to do—*the things that weren't fun or easy.*"

Patricia began to apply self-discipline to her life in a way she never had. Her grades improved. She soon saw that she could, in fact, do much better at everything when she applied self-discipline.

Then, suddenly, things took an unexpected turn for the Diaz family. Her sister, younger than she by one year, died when she was electrocuted by a radio that fell into the tub as she was bathing. This life-changing event opened Patricia's eyes. At seventeen, she learned that life is precious and fragile. "From that moment on, I never took anything for granted," she says. "I learned to enjoy the richness of life."

She also learned to balance self-discipline with the enjoyment of life. At an age when most of her friends were still wondering what life is all about, Patricia's life experiences had given her maturity far beyond her years. Her family's travels had given her an understanding of the beauty of different cultures. Her sister's passing had driven home the value of life. And Mrs. Smith's words had driven home the importance of self-discipline—a discipline she never forgot. A discipline that would become as much a part of her as breathing.

Then she met Michael Dennis, a young man of Swedish descent who would one day become her husband. Michael could see into Patricia's soul. He saw even more potential in the well-prepared and well-disciplined Patricia than even she could see. He noticed that she also had a facility for quick thinking. Because she was articulate, she could debate anyone on any subject. "These talents are worthy of a career in law, especially because you are winning all the arguments at home," he told her. That observation got her to thinking, and it got her on the road to the law degree that eventually resulted in her appointment as a vice president and legal counsel for the second largest telecommunications company in the United States.

The Big Four

If you want to apply the principle of self-discipline in the most useful and efficient ways, Napoleon Hill says to concentrate in these four areas:

1. Definiteness of purpose
2. Keeping a positive mental attitude
3. Eating right and keeping fit
4. Making good use of time

1. Definiteness of Purpose

When I first learned to establish my main definite purpose and set clear goals, I was amazed at how easily I could achieve anything I conceived and believed. In fact, I was so amazed, that the first few times I reached my goal, I forgot to make a new one.

When I achieved the goal of having my ad agency become the largest in Texas, I was so happy all I did for a while was glow about it. Then our growth stopped. "What happened? Why didn't we grow this year?" I asked after seeing flat billings several months in a row. The answer became obvious when I thought about it. I had not set a new goal after reaching my first one. I had expected the momentum to keep things moving.

It doesn't work that way. Continual growth and success doesn't happen automatically. *No puedes dejarle todo a Dios,* "You can't leave everything to God." Always think about your next goal. Don't let a day go by without thinking about it.

Setting and achieving new goals refreshes Patricia's journey toward her main definite purpose. She thrives on the recognition she gets, the new responsibilities she receives, and the increased trust she engenders from her colleagues. As soon as one of them is reached, she's off to the next. Don't be surprised if the next time you google her, you see an even more successful Patricia Diaz Dennis.

2. Keeping a Positive Mental Attitude

Think of your mental attitude as the home where your thoughts live. You have the power to send your thoughts to live in any of several homes. They will live wherever you say.

The first home is strong and made of beautiful stone. It can withstand any storm, even an earthquake. Outside, the yard is green and the flowers are blooming. Inside, everything is neat, clean, and in order. Here, things are warm and comfortable. If you instruct your thoughts to live here, they will be happy. They will also have the responsibility of working hard to keep their home beautiful, comfortable, and clean.

The second home is really a shack. It is barely standing. A strong wind could blow it over. The yard is tiny and overgrown with weeds. Inside, dirty dishes are piled to the ceiling. There is trash and garbage on the floor and furniture. Things don't smell particularly good. If you instructed your thoughts to live here, they wouldn't be very happy or have enough time for upkeep. In fact, they might sit around all day and complain about how bad things are.

The third home is really not a home at all. It is the street. Homeless folks push carts around aimlessly. They have no place to go. No appointments to keep. No responsibilities to live up to. Some are relatively happy here. Others are miserable but don't have a clue about how to get out.

The first home is where you want to be, of course. It is the home of a positive mental attitude. It is the home where your thoughts will be optimistic, comfortable, and directed toward your main definite purpose. Through self-discipline, you can direct your thoughts to this home. *With self-discipline you can keep them there.* It takes careful and steady concentration to do it, but it works every time.

3. Eating Right and Keeping Fit

I'm not a natural athlete. Never have been. Checkers is my sport. Keeping fit takes all the self-discipline I can muster. It's paying off. At age sixty-six, I can stay on the treadmill twice as long as the average forty-year-old. That's what my doctor, Jim Ogletree, observed when I got my last annual physical three months ago. I'm six feet tall, weigh 170 pounds, and still wear a nice wool Brooks Brothers suit I bought thirty years ago.

Most anyone can stay fit and healthy far into their eighties and nineties if they apply a little self-discipline to their daily routine. Just ask Jack Lalanne, the old guy selling juicers on TV. Jack is in his late nineties and is as trim, active, productive, and vigorous as any thirty-year-old. He works out three hours a day because that's his degree of self-discipline.

You needn't be as dedicated to working out as Lalanne, but if you follow a few sensible tips available in bookstores, in libraries, and on the Internet, you'll do just fine. Here's my routine. You can fashion your own.

Burn More Calories than You Eat

Enchiladas, empanadas, tostones, and such are okay, as long as the number of calories equal the number your physical activity burns up. A lot of people go from one diet to another, gaining and losing weight like a yo-yo. The fact is that you can eat small portions and still gain weight if you don't burn off more calories than you take in. A teenage boy on the basketball team can eat like a horse and still be trim because he burns up all the calories he takes in.

Be aware of your daily activity. If you have trouble with your weight, you are probably eating more than your physical activity is burning off. Get a cheap pedometer to count the steps you take in a day. If it's fewer than four thousand, you're probably not moving around enough to burn the calories you eat.

Walk, Jog, or Ride a Bike Thirty Minutes a Day

Do cardiovascular exercise first thing in the morning and get it out of the way. The important thing is to do it every day. It's no secret that the best exercise is the exercise you actually do. Many people think they exercise regularly but really do so only two or three times a week. That's not regular exercise. That's drive-by exercise. It won't help you lose weight. Or keep in shape.

Stretch and Lift Weights

Stretch twenty minutes each day to stay limber. Lift weights twenty minutes every other day to stay strong. It takes these two workouts along with your cardio to do the job. Cardiovascular, weights, and stretching—don't leave out one of these just because you may not like to do it. Remember, self-discipline means getting yourself to do the things you like to do as well as the things you don't like to do.

4. Making Good Use of Time

Napoleon Hill observed that most people spend enough time on *chismiando,* or on gossip, that if they were to spend it planning and doing good work, it would earn them all the luxuries for which they envy others. We must remember that he wrote this in 1937, when television was just being developed. If some people could reallocate the time they spend on gossip plus watching television, they could earn that fortune even more quickly today.

Some of us keep time sheets at work but not at home. I'm not suggesting that we should keep time sheets at home, yet it is a good idea to periodically and accurately analyze how you are using your time. If you are really honest, it may surprise you.

Not long ago, I was helping a young man figure out why he hadn't gotten better grades in his junior year in college. He is fully capable of making As and Bs but was falling a bit short. Once we did an hour-by-hour analysis of how he was spending his time, it became apparent that he was spending more hours socializing than attending class and studying.

We sat down and calculated how much time he was spending on such activities as calling and taking calls on his cell phone, time on dates or lining up dates, watching ESPN and reality shows, as well as time at the pub, at the student union, or at the dorm just "hanging out." We compared the total of that time to the time spent on actual schoolwork and summed up the hours. He was shocked to discover that although he was spending four-and-a-half hours a day in class (or studying), he was spending about ten hours a day in some sort of social activity. I advised him to make a small change in his schedule by cutting the social activities by two hours a day and transferring them to the study side. By doing that, he'll devote six-and-a-half hours to schoolwork and eight to the social activities. When he applies the self-discipline needed to reschedule his time, his grades will improve. He's a very smart and success-oriented young man.

The Structure of Your Mind

Napoleon Hill discovered that your mind is divided into six compartments. Each of these is totally controlled by you and you alone.

If you understand these compartments, he says, you will understand self-discipline. On the next several pages, you will see my adaptation of two charts that Napoleon Hill designed to illustrate this point. The first shows the compartments you can control and the other shows how they operate. If you want to see the originals just as he wrote them, please refer to his book *Napoleon Hill's Keys to Success,* pages 116 and 117.

The six compartments are ego, emotions, reason, imagination, conscience, and memory. Let me describe them in detail:

Ego

The dictionary defines ego as somebody's idea of his or her importance or worth. In Spanish, it's *el yo,* "the me." Napoleon Hill takes it to another level. He defines it as *the source of willpower.* Willpower so strong that it can change, reverse, or eliminate the work of any other department. Ego drives the decisions you make.

In Patricia Diaz Dennis's case, the source of her willpower is captured in her quote, "I want to be recognized for being the best at what I do. *I care about what people think of me and, more important, what I think of myself.*" She often quotes a thought she attributes to Theodore Roosevelt: "I care not what others think of what I do. But I care very much about what I think of what I do. That is character." Her desire to be recognized for doing the right thing fuels the self-discipline Patricia requires to consistently perform at her best.

Patricia is fully aware of the ego that drives her. She makes no apologies for it, and she shouldn't. *"Sé quien soy, Sé que me impulsa,"* she says, "I know who I am, I know what drives me." The validation she gets for working hard and doing the right thing satisfies her ego and drives her to the next goal. This self-understanding has led her to live a very successful and well-balanced life, one that includes a happy family and a remarkable career.

Many Latinos believe that ego is a bad thing. *"Es muy egoísta,"* they say. "He's an egoist." This immediately puts the ego in a negative context. Don't confuse the ego with the *overinflated* ego. Everyone has an ego. Some egos are weak and lacking in courage, says Mr. Hill. Others are overinflated. Most people and a majority of Latinos struggle with weak ones.

Check to see how your ego is doing. Do you get uneasy when you are in a strange new place or at a party with strangers who are more educated or wealthier than you? Do you get uneasy when the conversation turns to a subject you know nothing about? If it does, don't worry. It's normal. Just remember that your ego is nothing more than your own idea of your worth. Your own idea. Not anyone else's. That's why it is your willpower. It fuels the engine that drives you.

In January 2005, my wife Kathy and I attended President George W. Bush's second inaugural festivities. We had the privilege of being at a small dinner with Secretary of State Condoleezza Rice. Her Senate confirmation hearings had just concluded in her favor. As she stopped to chat at each table before dinner was served, I couldn't help but be amazed by her friendliness, comfort, and ease. She knows exactly who she is and what she is. She is a black woman from Alabama. And the nation's highest-ranking diplomat. And to my way of thinking, she has an ego in perfect balance.

Emotions

Your thoughts, your plans, and the actions you take toward accomplishing your main definite purpose are driven by your emotions. If your emotions are focused on desire, enthusiasm, faith, and hope, you will achieve your ultimate goal. If you let negative emotions such as fear, jealousy, greed, and revenge get in the way, I can guarantee you will not be successful. *Vas a quedar en la calle.* "You'll wind up on the street," as they say.

Remember when Patricia's younger sister was suddenly killed by electrocution? The whole Diaz household was overcome with emotion. Patricia and her sister were only a year apart in age and as close as could be. What if negative emotions had overtaken Patricia? What if her thoughts had been filled with superstition, anger, and revenge? Her life would have surely taken a different turn.

Instead, the family focused on whatever good could come from the terrible loss. The family talked about the love they felt for each other. And about the faith they had in infinite intelligence. These positive emotions led to a finer enjoyment of the richness of life and a deeper appreciation of one another as *familia*.

For Patricia it meant that she would never again take life for granted. *La vida se tiene que vivir,* "You gotta live life." Today, she never misses an opportunity to tell her children and her friends she loves them. "I try to make small moments magical. I work to make big memories happen on special occasions. Michael and I are on the same wavelength when it comes to enjoying life to the fullest with our children and extended family." It's true: positive emotions born of a positive attitude can overcome even life's biggest tragedies.

Reason

The familiar Spanish phrase, *Hay que tener razón,* "You must have reason," is a mantra many parents use in bringing up their children. Reason handles the more routine functions of judgment. When Mrs. Smith told Patricia not to settle for being mediocre, Patricia didn't feel hurt. She wasn't insulted. She didn't even challenge the observation. Patricia heard Mrs. Smith's message clearly, knew how she meant it, and took it all in. Instead of making a fuss, she reasoned that Mrs. Smith was right, that more effort would bring better results. And more recognition. She made the right decision, and it set her on course.

Conscience

Escucha a tu conciencia, "Listen to your conscience," is good advice. That little voice inside will always keep you honest. Only, however, if you learn to listen to it. It will always point out the difference between right and wrong. Trouble is, some people turn a deaf ear to it. They ignore it so often that they don't allow it to have a real influence. Patricia listens to her conscience. It gives her the confidence to make the good decisions that keep her life in balance.

Memory

Some people make a habit of holding on to unpleasant memories. Without noticing, their thoughts gravitate to unhappy events—*los tiempos de tristeza y dolor.* To the times when things didn't go their way. To the place where someone looked at them funny. *¿Qué miras?* "What you looking at?" was a favorite expression in my old neighborhood when some feisty *pachuco* wanted to start a fight. These people are allowing negative memory to keep them down.

Others have a natural ability to replace bad memories with good ones. If something bad or unpleasant happens, they don't let the event dominate their thoughts. They move on, learning from adversity and anticipating that something good will happen next.

Imagination

Imagine what would have happened to Patricia's future had she dwelled negatively on the memory of having been moved from school to school as she was growing up. Instead of complaining about it, as many would do, she took it in stride. Encouraged by her parents, she learned to appreciate the joy that comes from making new friends, learning about different cultures, and understanding proud traditions firsthand.

Patricia's memories and imagination have always had a way of gravitating toward the positive. As should yours. Take time at the end of each day to reflect on the memories you have chosen to remember. If they are good memories, your imagination will turn them into riches. If they are unpleasant memories, change them consciously through self-discipline. Make it a habit to consciously replace unpleasant memories with good ones. Imagine that good things will happen. And they will.

The Thing You Cannot Discipline

The chapters on the cosmic habitforce and on applied faith explain the power and importance of infinite intelligence. "You cannot discipline it," Napoleon Hill says, "instead you must discipline yourself to be ready to receive it and to act on its wisdom."

Controlled Attention
—Lionel and
Roberto Sosa

When you have a goal, you have the very thing you need to focus your controlled attention. A clear goal allows you to make the transition from weighing your options to making it happen. With a goal, all of your energy, all of your creativity, all of your experience, and all of your intelligence begin to turn ideas into reality. The ability to concentrate on a single idea is the beginning of all success. It is the foundation upon which everything else is built.

Controlled attention comes naturally to all of us at one time or another. Remember when you fell in love with that special someone? Remember when you said to yourself, "He's the one!" or "She's it!" You practiced controlled attention. You had a single goal: to win over your new love. There were no maybes. No ifs. You knew exactly what you wanted. You got creative. Ideas came to you as if by magic. You knew your plan would work. You had what Napoleon Hill called applied faith. You didn't give up when obstacles got in the way. And you got what you wanted.

Applying controlled attention to your life's goals doesn't come as naturally. It's a lot harder. There are so many options. So many possibilities. You may become afraid of putting all your eggs in one basket. You may fear making a mistake. But the biggest mistake you can make is to sit on the fence, to do nothing. When I see people in this state, I advise them to list their options, then to examine each one closely. Then I ask a question I learned from my good friend Charles Garcia: "What would you do if you knew you couldn't fail?" Think about it that way and the answer comes fast. And you know what? You won't fail if you follow Napoleon Hill's seventeen principles.

To make your goal a reality, you must train like an athlete trains for the Olympics. You must make a conscious effort to control your attention on *exactly what you want out of life.* The gold medal. My friend, that takes concentration. Effort. Work. It begins with a burning desire.

The desire to succeed is already in you. You wouldn't have read this far if it weren't. It's in you because of the lessons you've learned since you were small. When I think about the principle of controlled attention, I always remember certain experiences growing up. In many ways, my parents were slowly preparing me.

Lessons from Mamá y Papá

We learn more from our parents than we think we do. We learn even when we don't know what we're learning. The idea of controlled attention was inculcated into my brain by a series of family experiences that prepared me a little bit at a time. Sometimes our parents teach us by example. Other times by direct instruction. Parents who are really savvy take advantage of our youthful mistakes to drive home the lessons we remember throughout life.

My father, in his own quiet way, did just that. He taught me four big lessons that together led to my developing the ability to control my attention. My sense is that he was keenly aware of exactly what he was teaching. He made it a point to have me sit up and listen. He told me, over and over, the story of how he, his mother, and three siblings came to America.

From him, I learned four lessons that formed the components of controlled attention for me. I never forgot them:

1. *Buen juicio,* or "good judgment"
2. *Ser responsable,* or "personal responsibility"
3. *Trabajo duro y ser 'aguila,'* or "working hard and looking ahead"
4. *Confiar en gente,* or "trusting people"

Napoleon Hill used different phrases to describe the same traits. It was Mr. Hill who clarified the components of controlled attention and made them work for me. This is how he saw them:

1. Accurate thinking
2. Personal initiative
3. Creative vision
4. Attractive personality

1. Accurate Thinking

My first car was a four-door 1953 Hudson Hornet. It looked like a big green watermelon and I loved it. I was 18 years old, working, and living at home. To pay for my room and board, I gave Mom half of my weekly paycheck. *Qué lástima,* but "them was the rules" and Mom wouldn't bend, so there was no use in trying.

Even though I was single, I never had much money to spare. I was making minimum wage. Between car payments, gas expenses and repairs, and dating, it wasn't easy saving the money for a snazzy new set of shiny chrome wheel covers. But I did it. Eighty dollars! Probably a thousand in today's dollars. They looked great on my Hudson. So great, in fact, that they remained attached to my car all of three days. On the fourth night, someone stole them. I was furious. I had saved for months only to be left hubcapless. I moped and moped.

That evening at the local soda shop, I ran into a former schoolmate who was smart, cunning, and a prankster. When he heard my tale of woe, he had a solution.

"Let's go get another set tonight."

"You mean, steal a set?"

"*Claro.* Someone takes from you, you take from someone else. An eye for an eye. It's in the Bible."

In my anger, I swallowed his flawed logic and agreed. "Okay, we'll do it tonight."

We met at his house at midnight and trolled the streets of our west side neighborhood looking for a set of hubcaps as cool as mine. It was almost dawn before we found them.

"Stop here," I said.

I got out and ever so slowly and quietly took my tire tool and carefully removed all four covers and loaded them into the backseat of my Hudson. Amazingly, no one saw us. No dogs barked. No lights came on. No sirens blared. We were home free!

I put the covers on my car that very morning, secure in the knowledge that all was well with the world. After all, things were even-steven. The next day, however, my father noticed the different wheel covers. He was puzzled and wanted to know more.

"Damn," I thought. "Why did I make such a big deal about buying those things?"

Dad looked me straight in the eye. "These aren't your hubcaps. What happened?"

I froze. The truth blurted out before I could stop myself.

"I stole them last night but everything's cool. An eye for an eye, you know."

"Whose are they?"

"I have no idea. I'm not even sure what street we were on when we took them. It was late," I muttered.

"Take them off the car right now and meet me at seven-thirty tomorrow morning in the back alley with two wheel covers under each arm."

"Okay."

That night, I couldn't sleep. For the life of me, I couldn't understand what he was going to do at seven-thirty in the morning. Was he going to make me smash them? Was he going to drive over them with his car? Were we going to drive around, find the owner, and return the goods? How humiliating! I tossed and turned all night.

Bright and early the next morning, I reported to the appointed place at the appointed time, two shiny, gorgeous hubcaps under each arm.

"Stand right there. Look straight ahead," he said firmly, sounding like my ROTC drill team captain.

In a couple of minutes, I heard a big truck approaching. I looked to my right. It was the garbage truck. It stopped right in front of us.

"Give the man those covers."

Without a word, I handed over my heist. The garbage collector couldn't believe the gift.

"It's garbage," my father told him. "Take it away."

As the truck drove off, my father looked at me in a way I'll never forget and said, "That was wrong and dishonest and you know it. Never be dishonest again. All dishonesty gets you is garbage not worth having."

He walked away and never mentioned the incident again as

long as he lived. Inside, I knew I had done wrong. Yet I let my anger take over. It took my dad's lesson to jar me back into reality.

Dad would have called this lesson *buen juicio,* "learning good judgment." Napoleon Hill calls it accurate thinking. By either name, without it, you won't get far.

2. Personal Initiative

I told you earlier about how I borrowed the money to take Napoleon Hill's course, "The 17 Principles of Personal Achievement." This story illustrates a lesson in responsibility and personal initiative.

The cost of the course was two hundred and fifty dollars. A fortune for anyone in my position, the amount was more than I earned in a month and a half. I had no credit. I hadn't saved a dime. I couldn't borrow from Dad. For as long as I could remember, my father had been telling me firmly and often, "Once you're on your own, don't expect me to give you, or lend you *any* money. In any amount. So don't ask."

"I won't cosign for you at the bank either," he said after I asked anyway. "But I will go to the bank and ask my friend, Jim McCann, to loan you the money on your signature. Just make sure you pay him back. On or before the payment is due. Every month. Fair?"

"Fair."

Dad met me at the National Bank of Commerce and told Jim with confidence, "Lionel needs two hundred and fifty dollars to take a course I don't really understand. If you lend him the money, he'll pay you back on time. Lending him money will be as good as lending me money. Besides, he needs to start establishing bank credit here."

Jim smiled. "Robert," he said, "If you say your son's credit will be as good as yours, that's good enough for me. Lionel, sign here." Back then, banks made loans like that. No big loan committees. Just two men. Two friends. And their word.

I paid the loan back on time. It gave me the confidence and personal initiative to ask for other loans to keep growing the business. Jim McCann became my personal banker through the first ten years of Sosart, the best little art studio in town. Through him, more loans were available as the business grew. When he retired, he introduced me to Louie Lagledder, his replacement, who became my banking partner for the next ten years and helped Sosart become the biggest graphic design studio in Texas.

The bizarre experience of having my own father refuse to cosign my bank note was confusing and troubling. It bugged me for years. In my mind, it didn't make sense. It wasn't that he couldn't do it. He *wouldn't* do it.

As I got older, I understood. Dad was teaching me personal responsibility. And I learned something else: personal initiative. Napoleon Hill was right. To get what you ask for, you must be responsible. And show personal initiative.

3. Creative Vision and
4. Attractive Personality

This is the story I heard many times from my father. It is the story of how he, his mother, and his sisters came to America. It taught me Dr. Hill's lessons number three and four—creative vision and attractive personality.

In 1918, the revolution was raging in Mexico. My grandfather Fernando, his wife Cristina, and their four children were living in Mexico City (El Districo Federal). Fernando was a dashing, handsome merchant who provided well for his family. At the age of forty-eight, however, he contracted tuberculosis and died. The death of the family breadwinner, along with the instability caused by the war, wreaked havoc on the family. It took only a few months to deplete their savings. Cristina looked for work in town, but the menial jobs she was offered didn't pay enough to support her children. Soon they lost everything, even their home.

The solution? America and the American Dream of opportunity! Thousands of Mexican citizens, forced by the revolution to flee their homeland, were flocking across the border to Texas. They were finding jobs in the fields and on construction sites in the very place that had been part of their homeland less than three generations before. People spoke both Spanish and English in South Texas. Things were better here than in Mexico.

Cristina, thirty-two, was a strong and determined woman with fair skin. Her bloodline went back to Spain and Germany. Her children were young. Fernando, the oldest, was ten. Alicia was seven, Herlinda was six, and my father, Roberto, was three. Their first stop was a small town just across the Rio Grande—Eagle Pass, Texas. At first, stalwart Cristina eked out a living doing laundry for the neighbors. Then she remarried, but divorced after five years.

Once more, the family's survival was up to her. She set her creative vision on her next move, to the big city of San Antonio. There, the family found a house they could afford, a tiny bungalow on the poor side of town. The house bordered the black neighborhood. To the west were the burgeoning Mexican neighborhoods. The middle-class Anglo families lived to the north.

By the time the family settled in San Antonio, the children were old enough for school. And for work. Cristina, by now thirty-seven and tough as ever, took a big risk. She would start her own business, a "home laundry." After school, her children, including the seven-year-old who would become my father, walked the neighborhoods door-to-door picking up people's laundry. The promise? To wash and press each item—shirts, pants, underwear, you name it—and return them to the customer's doorstep clean, ironed, and folded the next evening.

After supper each day, when the laundry had been collected,

the family would wash all the clothes and hang them out to dry. Early the next morning, Cristina starched and ironed each piece. She worked until 1 or 2 p.m., and then took an afternoon siesta (a custom I wish still prevailed). When the children came home after school, they had a quick snack and then went off to deliver laundry and pick up new orders.

The business did well because the entire family controlled its attention on doing the laundry well. They stuck to it. It made enough money to feed and clothe the family, even as they got older. When my father was ten, his own creative vision kicked in. He had saved enough pennies from the tips he got to buy a bicycle with a big basket in front. With it, he could ride as far as he needed to find customers with greater disposable income. He figured that people with more money had more clothes. And more laundry to send out.

The black and Mexican neighborhoods were close by and easier to service. But the people who lived there were also the poorest and least likely to pay to have someone wash and iron their clothes. Now my father began doing business with the people who had money: the Anglos. That was creative vision.

From then on, he rode his bike every day to the swankiest neighborhoods in town. He must have had a very attractive personality, even as a teen, because he converted some of San Antonio's most influential people into good and steady customers. Dad discovered something else. These people also had boatloads of dry cleaning that the home laundry couldn't service. As he got older, the idea of setting up his own laundry and cleaners became a burning desire. He started saving his quarters with the goal of being able to do this when he turned twenty-one.

Sure enough, it happened. It happened because he had used controlled attention, creative vision, and a pleasing personality. On his twenty-first birthday, he opened the doors to the new and pristine "Prospect Hill Laundry and Cleaners" in an all-Anglo, mostly German neighborhood. As I think back, I marvel at his instincts.

He didn't name it the "Sosa Laundry and Cleaners." That might not have worked in a day when segregated neighborhoods were the norm. As the only Mexican businessperson there, he saw no need to call special attention to the fact. Instead, he named his business after the neighborhood, Prospect Hill. To that, I say, "Good call, old man," even though he was a young man then. A very young man.

Mom and Dad married the same year and set up their first home in the back room of the shop, alongside the dry-cleaning fluids, hot water boiler, and washtubs. The Sosas were the only Mexican family to own a business in Prospect Hill and the only Mexican family to live there.

Was Roberto Sosa asking for trouble? Of course not! He was doing what came naturally—doing business with the people who had the most money. His customers were Mr. Jones, Mr. Gibson, Reverend Brown, Mr. Kappmeyer, and Mrs. Burkholder. His employees were Jesse and Tex McLeod. To all of them, he was Mr. Sosa. How he loved being called Mr. Sosa. He had known many of his customers for ten years—some since he was eleven years old. They loved him and he loved them. Because trust was developed through friendships, we saw each other as friends, not as Mexicans and Anglos. The ethnic issue never reared its ugly head. Not once that I remember.

Growing up in an all-Anglo neighborhood had a great effect on me. It made me understand the value of expecting to be treated equally. I never thought of an Anglo as different. Or as better. I didn't experience discrimination because I didn't expect it. I have always been proud of being a Mexican. Of being Latino. But like most Latinos, I'm just as proud of being an American. An equal American.

I tell these stories in hopes of prompting you to think back to your childhood and recollect the wisdom inherent in your family histories and in our rich Latino culture. Combine them with the teachings of Napoleon Hill and make it work for you. Through controlled attention.

Note: Today, the neighborhood in San Antonio, Texas, known as Prospect Hill is 99 percent Latino. Henry Cisneros, former HUD secretary, says that more national U.S. Latino leaders have come from this area than from any other in America.

Inspiring Teamwork
—Jeff Valdez
and Bruce Barshop

We have learned through Napoleon Hill's teachings that it is practically impossible to achieve great success single-handedly. The laws of nature seem to prohibit success in isolation. To help you reach your definite purpose, you will need a team with you.

This team is not to be confused with the mastermind alliance. As we know from chapter 2, the mastermind alliance is a small group, usually two or three people, working in perfect harmony toward the same goal. The team works hand in glove with the alliance and can be small or large. It consists of salaried employees and perhaps a trusted accountant, lawyer, banker, or other key supplier. This team must understand the goal of the mastermind alliance and be committed to achieving it.

How do you inspire teamwork? How do you keep your team working together, especially when things get tough? I got the answer from Jeff Valdez and Bruce Barshop, the mastermind alliance behind the creation of SíTV. They put together the first and only twenty-four-hour English-language television cable channel aimed at Latinos in the United States.

They hired our ad agency to develop their advertising and sales materials, so I witnessed these developments firsthand. This may sound like a story of sheer determination and focus by two people, but it's really a story about team building. When you read it, you'll understand why.

It took six years to get SíTV on the air. For seventy-two straight months, Jeff, Bruce, and their team of employees, investors, and an investment banker labored tirelessly to achieve what others hardly understood, much less supported. The idea of a 24/7 television channel targeted to Latinos, in English rather than Spanish, proved to be a very hard sell. Advertisers were skeptical, asking, "Don't most all Latinos watch Spanish TV?" Their next question was usually, "If it's in English, how do I know Latinos are watching?"

Madison Avenue ad agencies were not any more supportive. They wanted hard numbers. "How many people will be watching and who exactly will they be?" The Hispanic ad agencies were nervous because they consider their assignment to be Spanish media. Satellite cable carriers, such as DirectTV, who would eventually carry their programming to millions of Latino homes, were also confused. They were unsure whether SíTV would add real value to their programming package. They were unconvinced that local cable companies would welcome SíTV to the lineup. And, worse, they were doubtful that SíTV could deliver top-quality programming 24/7.

All of these are good questions. Some would call them insurmountable barriers. Nevertheless, Jeff and Bruce had a plan. They had answers as well. Their main selling job was to convince everyone that their concept was both doable, valuable, and worthy of their confidence. They began by putting together their business plan, profit projections, and prospectus. To succeed, they would have to change a lot of minds.

So they designed a top-notch sales presentation outlining the opportunity. It is common knowledge that 75 percent of Latinos in the United States watch Spanish television. What was not widely known is that 75 percent of Latinos watch it in English as well. This is because 75 percent of Latinos are bilingual and consume their media in both languages. Only 25 percent watch Spanish TV *exclusively.* These facts confirmed the durable opportunity for SíTV, especially because *the longer a Latino lives in the United States the more he or she watches in English.*

I don't mean to give you a lesson in Hispanic media, just an idea of the challenge and the opportunity Jeff and Bruce faced. Their business plan was to be up, running, and on the air in two years. It took three times that. Those six years were tough. To them it felt like twenty. It wasn't just the long days, nights, and weekends at the office and on the road that made their journey so arduous. It was the money being sucked out and needing to be replenished by the investors, week after week. Several times, they came within hours of closing a deal, only to see it evaporate at the last minute.

What Is Teamwork?

Jeff and Bruce would not be denied. When I asked them what kept the team going over so many months, given the obstacles and disappointments they faced, the men answered in unison: "Vision and focus."

The SíTV team consisted of a few key employees, a handful of consultants, and a dogged investment banker. "We had this consistent vision to keep the team together—to finish the triathlon all the way to the finish line no matter what it took," Jeff explained. Bruce continued the thought without missing a beat. "When we came to a brick wall, we stopped, made changes, and started all over again. Reaching a destination is like steering down a straight road—you gotta move the wheel a little, or you'll eventually drive off."

He continued, "Our goal was to get SíTV on the air. We never took our eye off that ball. We never lost faith in our idea. Our belief in our definite purpose is the very thing that built the team. It also kept it motivated and running on all eight cylinders."

The SíTV model is a perfect example of how Napoleon Hill described teamwork:

> Teamwork comes directly from the mastermind alliance—a small group committed to the same definite purpose and who share the same burning obsession. Each of them benefits from the other's enthusiasm, imagination and knowledge. Further, they are in agreement on the division and rewards of their labor.

"Teamwork," he continued, "establishes much the same relationship, but since it involves working with people who probably don't have the same burning obsession you do, it requires more effort on your part to maintain their commitment to your work."

The more commitment you show, the more commitment your team will have. Management guru Peter Drucker said that all employees need to see themselves as executives. Donald Trump writes that every team member must feel that they are making a difference. Both are correct. When team members feel they are contributing to a worthwhile goal, they will take ownership of your dream and work in earnest to help you achieve it.

Commitment Inspires Teamwork

"Could we handle the word 'no'? Bruce and I asked ourselves this question after the tenth rejection to our sales pitch," Jeff explained. "We were riding in a cab one day in New York City on our way to a call, when we realized that we could point to more buildings on the skyline that had turned us down than we could to those we could still call on."

At this point, early in 2002, Jeff and Bruce had been at it for three years. September 11 had changed the investment world. The stock market had crashed and the country was nervous. Potential suitors were not in the mood to take risks. SíTV was a year behind schedule. Money was getting impossible to come by. The team was growing disheartened. A few quit, fearing the worst.

Most ordinary people would have thrown in the towel right about then. They had real reason to do so. But these guys wouldn't quit. "To keep going, sometimes we would joke, 'Let's see who's going to turn us down today,' " Jeff told me. "We had to keep our sense of humor in the midst of it all. No one had ever tried to do what we were doing, we reasoned. Maybe we aren't really a year behind schedule. Maybe it was supposed take much longer."

Bruce chimed in, "One person who didn't quit was our banker, Andy Franklin, with Citicorp. He told us recently, 'You guys were so committed, I *couldn't* leave the team.' "

Commitment Begins at Home

As we all know, Latinos are extremely family focused. Many times one or more of our family members are part of the team or of our mastermind alliance. The feelings of our spouse or significant other should always be considered. Even when they're not part of the official organizational chart, they influence one's success.

When SíTV was going through the worse of times, Jeff Valdez asked his wife, "What if this thing doesn't work out? What if we lose everything?" She replied, "The day you get tired of this, or can't go on, I will be there. If we have to live in a trailer park, we will. As long as we have each other and the kids, we'll be just fine."

Maria's lovely commitment gave Jeff the strength to carry on. He'd been traveling from Los Angeles to New York and points in between weekly. His time at home was getting rare. Even when in town, he worked late nights so often that his office was doubling as a bedroom. It was no wonder that he needed her reinforcement.

Commitment Comes from Purpose

Another thing kept Jeff going: a deep passion for Latino equality in the media. He longed to see Latinos depicted on English television as "normal people." We must remember that up to a few years ago, Hispanics were virtually absent from English network and cable television. When they appeared, they were usually cast as bandits, drug dealers, and hoodlums. This, in spite of the fact that millions of middle-income, well-educated Latinos populate our country.

"I didn't want my kids to grow up watching TV never having seen themselves. That's not good for their self-image. I don't want them wondering whether or not they belong. I wanted to create a *nidito,* a "nest" or "television home," where Latinos can see themselves as contemporary citizens of their country living all aspects of the American Dream, good and bad."

Bruce is a Texan by birth, Jeff is a Californian by choice. Bruce is white, Jeff is brown. Bruce is a Princeton man, Jeff didn't go to college. Bruce is a businessman, Jeff is a comedian. Bruce is a staunch conservative. Jeff is a yellow-dog liberal. Despite all these differences, they are as together as any two partners could be. They understand the Latino market and Latino media consumption. Most of all, they understand the doors media can open for so many.

Today, SíTV is a reality. It is on the air and enjoyed in more than 8 million American homes. By the time this book is published, the figure will top 10 million. Fortune 500 advertisers are on its client list. Many of the folks who doubted the concept at the beginning are now part of the team, among them Dish Network, their primary carrier, as well as major ad agencies, both general market and Hispanic. And, of course, their investment banker, Andy.

Keeping the Team Motivated

When I was in business, I made sure every member of my team understood the company's goal to be the biggest and the best Hispanic agency in the country. I also made sure that everyone had plenty of room to implement their ideas toward achieving the goal. Each year, our top management team set the bar a little higher with new strategies. The middle management team helped work out the action items to make them happen.

Everyone at the agency had a responsibility. People were rewarded based on performance and overall profits. They were recognized for their special contributions. Those who performed beyond expectations were given special praise and recognition at monthly gatherings and at the annual Christmas party. We also praised our best suppliers and regarded them not as vendors, but as special members of the team.

The entire agency met every Monday morning to catch up on the latest happenings, review assignments, share our accomplishments and fiascos, celebrate births, weddings and birthdays, and so on. Most importantly, I kept them believing what I believed. That we were destined to become the biggest and the best Hispanic advertising agency in America. Bigger and better than any in New York. Bigger and better than any in Los Angeles.

Did we do it? Yes, we did. Just like SíTV. We had something in common—our team believed we could!

TWENTY TIPS ON BUILDING AND KEEPING YOUR
TEAM TOGETHER

1. Have a clear goal—a definite purpose.
2. Write it down—have a date for its completion.
3. Assemble your mastermind alliance.
4. Make sure you don't overlap responsibilities.
5. Write a business plan (see chapter 10).

6. As soon as you need them, assemble your team.
7. Communicate your goal to them clearly and often.
8. Give them each a specific job description.
9. Tell them what to do, not how to do it.
10. Give them the tools they need.
11. Encourage them—cheer them on.
12. Let them make a difference.
13. Recognize their good work.
14. Reward their efforts.
15. Celebrate victories and accomplishments.
16. Be fair and consistent—don't pick favorites.
17. Keep them focused on the goal.
18. Give them real responsibility.
19. Make them accountable.
20. Improve the strategies—keep the goal.

Accurate Thinking
—Raymund Paredes

"Your mind is like a piece of land you own," Napoleon Hill says. "It can become a beautiful garden full of flowers. Or it can lie fallow and be overrun with weeds that sprout from the seeds carried from passing birds and the wind." I like that metaphor. As the gardener of your own mind, you have two choices. If you choose a garden full of beautiful flowers, lush plants, and greenery, you will be choosing to invest the time and other resources needed to tend your garden, feed it, water it, and keep the bad bugs away.

Your second option is to leave the land alone, not worry about it, and see what happens. Maybe it'll rain often enough. Maybe pretty wildflowers will grow on their own. Maybe the neighbor will tend to it. Watch out, though—your piece of land will most likely grow weeds. If you're thinking accurately, you will choose the first option. You already own the land. Go for it. Why not grow something beautiful to have and enjoy?

In his day, Napoleon Hill didn't have the pleasure of knowing too many Latinos or he might have identified a third option. Those among us who struggle with accurate thinking consider it, often quite unconsciously. Using the garden metaphor, the inner dialog goes something like this:

> I'm not sure I should plant on this land. What if I lose it? Besides, I'm not a good enough gardener. The stuff I planted in my other house died. What if I can't afford to feed and care for the garden regularly? Why set myself up for failure? I'd like to have a big beautiful lush garden but I'm not sure.

What they're really thinking, without knowing it, is, "I'd like to have a big beautiful lush garden *but I'm not sure I deserve it.*"

That's a prime example of inaccurate thinking. Anyone who truly wants success deserves to have it. Do you deserve success? Of course you do. Yes you do. Yes you do. Of course you do!

But . . .

You must believe you deserve success before you can have it. You must believe you deserve it with every ounce of your being. You must be convinced that nothing will stand in your way. Napoleon Hill said it. I say it. "Whatever your mind can conceive and believe, you can achieve."

But . . .

You won't even get to first base if you don't believe you deserve success. Why? Because you won't be able to truly *conceive* of success. You will only wish for it. You will not be able to *believe* you'll be successful. You will only *hope* you will.

Convincing Yourself You Deserve Success

Believing you deserve success is the first step in thinking accurately. If you want to think accurately, make up your mind now that you deserve it. Accurate thinking means you know you will not go to hell if you become rich. Accurate thinking means you know you are not a bad person if you want to be fabulously successful. Or incredibly famous.

Remember that success means different things to different people. To Mother Teresa, success was helping the helpless. She was incredibly famous and it helped her do her job. To film director Alejandro Amenabar success is making a great unforgettable movie and winning an Academy Award. To former HUD secretary, Henry Cisneros, it is building affordable, high-quality homes for first-time homebuyers. To you, it may be getting a college degree or starting your own business. It may be making a hundred million bucks. Whatever your goal, to achieve it you must first believe you deserve to achieve it.

For some Latinos, believing we deserve success comes easy. For many others, it comes hard. This is at least partly because a strong dose of inaccurate thinking was forced into our forefathers' minds over five hundred years ago when the conquistador convinced the native Indian not to desire riches. If they did, they were taught they might risk going to hell. "God loves the poor. If you are poor, your road to heaven will be easier." This brainwashing was a convenient way to keep the conquered peoples in their place. The trouble is that some of us still carry that belief deep in our subconscious.

Religion and Personal Achievement

It is no secret that countries with high percentages of Catholics are poorer than those with high percentages of Protestants. The reasons are clear. The Catholic religion teaches humility, sacrifice, frugality, and the virtues of the common man. It does not encourage the accumulation of personal wealth or the idea of personal achievement.

Protestantism is grounded on a vastly different set of principles. The words "Protestant" and "work ethic" are often used in the same context. Hard work and the dedication toward achievement are encouraged. Calvinistic Protestants promoted the idea that wealth is a good thing. And that men and women who have acquired it must have been selected by God to improve their piece of the world. They also taught that those God selected have an obligation to work to improve it.

Latinos have been aligned with the Catholic Church for centuries. La Reina Isabel, queen of Spain, who financed Cristobal Colón's discovery of America, had an interesting name. Isabel, la Católica.

Today, a new trend is emerging: the growth of Protestant Latinos. As recently as twenty-five years ago, there were only one hundred thousand Latino Protestants in the United States. Now, there are five million: a growth of 5,000 percent! One of these people worthy of note is Raymund Paredes, the Texas commissioner of higher education. He's the one who opened my eyes to this changing paradigm.

Can Religion Influence Accurate Thinking?

This is a question that has been argued by intellectuals, philosophers, theologians, and scholars for centuries. This is a mystery that perhaps has no answer. What we will do is surface some thoughts and theories worthy of your time and consideration.

"*Cómo está la Católica?*" Loosely translated, this means, "What are the Catholics up to now?" This was the question Raymund's father asked facetiously when he called his son at UCLA when he heard that a big Latino student hunger strike was in full swing. As dean of the graduate school there, Raymund was the highest-ranking Latino in the administration. It was an awkward position to be in, but he took it in stride. Raymund looked out his window at the students carrying the hand-scrawled signs and answered with a sigh, "*Tienen mucha fe, Dad,* 'they've got a lot of faith, Dad.' "

Raymund had been dealing with the reality of being the odd man out all his life. He grew up a double minority. A Latino and a Protestant. His grandmother on his father's side had founded La Primera Iglesia Bautista Mexicana in her hometown of El Paso, Texas, back in 1892. The First Mexican Baptist Church was not only her creation, it was her pride and joy. As a young woman of eighteen, she went to a Baptist revival and converted on the spot. The Protestant services and gatherings were more joyful and fulfilling than the more somber Catholic goings-on. Besides, she could understand the Spanish Baptist services a lot better than she could the Latin Catholic mass.

When she married and had a family, she and her husband raised their children as Baptists. Their youngest, Abel Junior, who was to become Raymund's father, became a Baptist of high stature.

Abel Paredes and his wife, Josefina, who converted from Catholicism when they married, were committed to the faith. They were also strict. If the kids shirked church, there would be nothing else. No play. No TV. No nothing. On Sunday, it was Sunday school, Sunday sermon, and Sunday night service. There was vacation Bible school every summer. The routine was not drudgery to Raymund and his brother and sisters. It was just the way things were. *Así son las cosas.*

Mom read the Bible every night to her children. Raymund's earliest memories are of his mom, he, and his brother Abel in bed, as she read the children's version of the Bible to them. These stories had pictures, adventure, drama, and suspense. Jonah and the whale, Daniel in the lion's den, and of course Cain and Abel (not his brother's favorite). The nightly readings had a profound effect on Raymund. He developed a love for reading and literature from them as well as an appreciation for the beauty and power of words. At Sunday services when the preacher walked up to the lectern, he stood for a few seconds. When he opened the Bible, the congregation stood up at once. To the young Raymund, this demonstrated the sacredness and importance of the written word.

By the time Raymund got to school, he could read in both English and Spanish. He was skipped from the first grade to the third. His father bought the family an *Encyclopedia Britannica,* though he couldn't really afford it. Raymund loved it and spent hours devouring its contents. He became aware that there was a world outside his neighborhood.

When he was about twelve and started making friends outside the family, he began to notice that most of the other kids were Catholic and did things rather differently. The most significant difference he noticed was the role of the priest as the intervener between God and the faithful. He noticed other differences.

Catholics confessed their sins to the priest.
Baptists confessed directly to God.
Catholics prayed to Nuestra Señora de Guadalupe.
Baptists prayed to God.
Catholics had Holy Water.
Baptists did not.
Catholics could drink liquor.
Baptists shouldn't.
Catholics could go to dances.
Baptists shouldn't.
Catholics showed Christ suffering on the cross.
Baptists showed only the cross.
Catholics made the sign of the cross.
Baptists bowed their heads.
Catholics celebrated the day of the dead.
Baptists celebrated life.
Catholics had Quinceañeras as a coming out.
Baptists simply turned fifteen.
Catholics celebrated El Dia de su Santo.
Baptists had no assigned saints. No saints at all.

These differences were discussed at length at the Paredes dinner table. A friendly banter developed when the conversation turned to us and them, *ellos y nosotros.* The Paredes family was not about to let their choice of religions make them feel "less Mexican." Among them, they made a case for *our way is the proper way.*

"The *Católicos* worship death, we worship life. We don't celebrate a dead Christ; we celebrate the God who lives among us. We don't celebrate sorrow. We celebrate happiness." These conversations reinforced their belief that in their religion, they could feel comfortable having an attitude of confidence and optimism. And because Baptists were accustomed to having to "make their own case" directly to God through prayer, they were better prepared to deal with reality. "If you're going to make your own case, it better be a good one," Raymund's father would say.

The family's favorite *dicho* is *Ayúdate, que Dios te ayudará,* "God helps those who help themselves." It was not the phrase more commonly used among Latino Catholic families, *Lo que Dios quiera,* "Whatever God wants." If Raymund, his brother, or sisters experienced discrimination, their father would say, "Deal with it." The Paredes kids were taught to be *hombrecitos,* real men who defend themselves. "Always be respectful, defend yourself against bullies, and never act humble. Humility is not a virtue!" I agree with that. Many of us think of humility as a virtue but others see it as subservience.

At this point, if you're a Catholic you may be wondering, "Are you telling me I have to become a Protestant to think accurately?" Of course not! Countless successful Latinos today are Catholic. There will be thousands more in the future. Just understand there are lessons to be learned from Raymund's Protestant upbringing.

Don't expect an intermediary to make the case for you. That's your responsibility. No one else's.

Don't put too much importance on suffering. You don't have to suffer to succeed.

Don't confuse humility and modesty with subservience.

Don't accept continuous struggle as a given.

Don't equate poverty with goodness.

Don't view wealth as evil or unethical.

Paredes observes that there are many factors other than your religion that can contribute to accurate thinking. He rattles them off:

1. *The support and encouragement of family.* Children who grow up with parental support, even if it's from one parent, will have greater confidence and a stronger sense of self.

2. *The support of education by parents* and the knowledge of the difference a college education can make. For example, a college graduate earns two million dollars more than a high school dropout over a lifetime. That's two million times better than winning *la lotería* because you're guaranteed to win the prize.

3. *An entrepreneurial spirit.* Children who come from families who had or have their own business develop a sense of optimism, responsibility, and pride of ownership. Earning one's living and creating wealth.

4. *Hard work.* This trumps native intelligence every time. If you work hard enough, you can do anything. Many of the things we consider genius are really the result of good old-fashioned hard work. Many people who are perceived as exceptionally intelligent are really exceptionally hardworking people of average intelligence.

5. *A habit of saving and investing.* The value of building equity should not be underestimated. Spending less than you take in and saving and investing part of every check is key to accurate financial thinking and long-term security.

6. *Appreciation of our bilingual and bicultural heritage.* You can take this advantage to the bank. This facility enables us to better understand others and ourselves. It's an ever more important key to success in the twenty-first century.

7. *The ability to shrug off discrimination* and take responsibility for your own future. You become a knee-jerk victim when you blame every bad thing that happens on discrimination.

Developing Accurate Thinking

The way you think affects your decisions. Your decisions drive your success. That's why accurate thinking is so vital. Accurate thinking nets you a higher percentage of good decisions. The more good decisions you make, the sooner you will realize your goal.

In making our everyday decisions, each of us tends to fall into a style or pattern. Some prefer to trust their instincts and make gut decisions with information already in hand. Others prefer to gather information, being careful to weigh all the alternatives carefully.

In his bestselling book *Blink,* author Malcolm Gladwell tells us that either of the two methods is as likely to produce a good decision. He describes how people, over and over again, come to the same conclusion regardless of the time exposed to a problem or situation. Test results have proved it. People tend to arrive at the same decision whether they take in months of information or minutes of it. In other words, time has little to do with how accurately we think.

As much as anything, accurate thinking comes from being aware of what's going on around you. People who think accurately have the ability to tell:

1. The *truth* from the lie
2. The *real* from the fake
3. The *right* from the wrong

4. The *important* from the insignificant
5. The *great idea* from the lame idea

Some people know immediately when something doesn't feel right. They can smell something fishy a mile away. Others can't smell it even when it's right under their nose. Some people can instantly decide whom they can or can't trust. Others never learn. Some folks know when to bet on the cards they're holding. And when to fold. Others get bluffed every time.

This phenomenon is called intuition, or the sixth sense. It's a great advantage to have in making decisions. But what is it? Is it an innate talent within you? Or a learned ability? It's really both. It's there. All you have to do is listen. Trust it. And hone it. People who have this sense

- Genuinely like people, empathize with them, and work to understand their hopes, dreams, and motivations
- Listen attentively. They remember what is said and who said it
- Carefully observe and internalize the details of events, large and small
- Study body language and understand the nuances of the way people stand, sit, gesture, and move
- Are open to the ideas of others and welcome different points of view
- Are confident in their decisions and don't second-guess themselves
- Believe their decisions will result in success
- Believe they deserve success.

In sum, intuitive people are in touch. They are in touch with other people and with the world around them. They don't build walls to protect themselves from the outside. As a result, they are able to receive important cues and signals that lead them, consciously or unconsciously, to wise decisions.

Controlled Habits

Napoleon Hill repeatedly emphasized that your thoughts are the only thing over which you can exert complete control. That's true. Still, you must be aware of the fact that there are thinking patterns you inherit that affect the way you think. They come from three places:

1. *Cultural heredity and history.* Ours is the Latino culture and history. In this book, I've described them based on my twenty-five years of research. In countless ways, our culture and history help us to be better people. In other ways, they hinder our ability to achieve our goals. Don't make the mistake of assuming that this history influenced only past generations. After conducting focus group research among young Latinos at risk just recently, I find that our troubled youth still carry a lot of old cultural baggage. Just like their fathers and grandfathers, these kids believe that dropping out of school and getting any job is the best way to help the family.

2. *Physical heredity.* One side of your brain almost always functions more effectively than the other. If your left side is dominant, math, science, and attention to detail will come easier. If your right side is dominant, art, music, and writing will be your thing. You can learn to make the most of your natural abilities, for example, by leaving the things that aren't as easy for you to a member of your mastermind alliance.

3. *Social heredity.* Where you grew up, what your parents did, and how much you were loved or encouraged will have an effect on your outlook on life. How you feel about discrimination or being part of a minority population will also impact your think-

ing and attitude. If you pay too much attention to the negative, it can become a problem because you may buy in on the notion that other people and outside influences are driving your life.

In this chapter, there's a lot to take in. A lot to ponder. Don't try to digest all of its contents at one time. You may want to reread it many times over. With each reading, you may find the seed of a new idea. And a new way to improve the accuracy of your thinking.

Learning from Adversity
—Phil Fuentes

In every defeat you experience, there is an equivalent benefit. Remember that truth. You will learn from it if you embrace it. It is an observation first made in the 1930s by Napoleon Hill and, as far as I know, no one has repudiated it—least of all those who have achieved great success.

The key word in Mr. Hill's observation is the word "equivalent." Every defeat has an equivalent benefit. If you think about that statement and accept it as fact, you will never again be paralyzed or even slowed down by the thought of possible defeat or failure. How could you? If you experience a temporary setback, you are sure to derive an equivalent benefit. All you have to do is look for it. It's always there in a lesson to be learned. So what is there to be afraid of? Nothing! Yet many people never take the first step toward success for dreadful fear of failing.

Everyone Encounters Defeat

It is impossible to achieve great success without experiencing defeat. No one is exempt. Even superstars like the beautiful Jennifer Lopez have had their share of bombs. Not only in movies, such as the two-thumbs-down *Gigli,* but also in her romantic relationships.

Henry Cisneros, one of the most admired Latinos in America, had his term in office plagued by personal scandal while serving as a cabinet member for President Clinton. Today, he is as revered as ever, both in his community and in corporate America. Henry bounced back to earn millions and to serve the places where he lives and does business. Today he is head of several companies. The biggest of them, American CityVista, builds new starter homes in renovated inner-city parcels of land other developers overlooked. He created the not-for-profit American Sunrise to educate and inspire at-risk youth and their families. Learning from adversity, the amazing Mr. Cisneros is doing better than ever.

Cruz Bustamante, California's lieutenant governor, lost a hard-fought gubernatorial race in 2004 to Arnold Schwarzenegger. I chatted with him after the race, and judging from his strength of character my guess is that he'll be back.

If you accept defeat as merely a test of your commitment, you will learn from it. You will become smarter and stronger on your journey to your definite major goal. "Remember," Napoleon Hill said, "defeat is not failure unless and until you accept it as such. Defeat is not a benefit in and of itself. It is only the seed from which benefit may be coaxed."

Adversity Becomes a Blessing

When Phil Fuentes was six months old, his parents noticed that their happy baby wasn't moving quite as easily as others his age. His right side wasn't as mobile as his left side. They took him to the

Children's Memorial Hospital in Chicago, where he was diagnosed with a rare form of cerebral palsy. His lifelong treatment began early in childhood, often with daylong trips to the neighborhood clinic. His mother would pack a lunch; they would take a bus, take a number, and then wait a couple of hours to begin therapy.

While he was in the second grade at St. Bartholomew Elementary School, doctors recommended that young Phil be put in a special school for children with disabilities. His mother would not hear of it. "As Phil gets older, he will have to adapt to the world and society," she declared. "I want there to be no boundaries for my son. He must be able to do all he can with no one holding him back."

Mrs. Fuentes talked the principal at St. Bart's into allowing her son to stay there while continuing his daily occupational and physical therapy. Starting at the age of eight, Phil began a series of surgeries that were to occur every summer for four years. There were no summer vacations for the family during that time. This was a bit of a downer for his two brothers and little sister, who were always ready to go on holiday.

Phil's physical limitations were apparent. His right elbow and hand seemed invisibly strapped close to his body—his fist always clenched. He walked with a noticeable limp, planting his left foot with the right one pointing in. One leg was shorter than the other. He didn't have bones on the tips of his fingers. His hand didn't have the strength to grasp. None of these things stopped Phil from wanting to do everything the other kids could do, like riding a bike—a skill he finally mastered in the sixth grade.

"People were always trying to tell me what I could do and what I couldn't do," Phil explained. "I'm realistic. I know I'll never play center for the Chicago Bulls. But I do know this much. If I don't try to do what I've never done, I'll never know."

That phrase became his mantra. He repeated it to himself every time an obstacle came his way. "If I don't try, I'll never know." He repeated it to those who tried to put obstacles in his way. "If you don't let me try, you'll never know." This was an attitude that became deeply engrained in his consciousness. Phil learned it from his parents. "I can't remember them keeping me from doing anything I set my mind to do. Whether it had to do with riding a bike or having a paper route. From Mom and Dad I learned that adversity could be a blessing. I had cerebral palsy. I never let it defeat me."

Defeat him it didn't. Today Phil Fuentes is a highly visible and successful owner-operator of some of the highest-volume McDonald's restaurants in Chicago. His stores consistently rank in the top 10 percent nationally. He won his company's highest award for service and presided over Phil Fuentes Day in the Chicago suburb of Cicero, where he owns and operates two McDonald's restaurants.

When Phil was just sixteen, he met stockbroker Jim Olsen, the man who introduced him to Napoleon Hill's philosophy and who would become his lifelong friend and mentor. Phil's older brother had been dating Olsen's secretary and introduced the two. They struck up a friendship immediately. Olsen was impressed with Phil's sunny outlook and can-do attitude, and decided to take him under his wing. He started giving Phil business advice. "Invest in the stock market," he said. "McDonald's restaurants are a good buy."

Phil took every dollar of savings he had been squirreling away and invested five hundred dollars in the growing restaurant chain. That was a lot of money for a teenager, but he trusted Olsen, so he did it. As you can conclude, this early decision would have a major effect on his later life.

The Benefits of Defeat

Every time Phil made a decision to take a new bold step into the job market, someone was there to say, "You can't do this," or "You mustn't try that," or "Don't even think about it." This type of steady rejection would have been enough to defeat most people. Not Phil. His response was always, "If you don't let me try, you'll never know." All the time he was saying to himself, "If I don't try, I'll never know."

Each job interview could have ended in defeat. Even the tough job as skycap at Chicago's O'Hare International Airport, a position he held for eleven years. When he first applied, the response was, "Not qualified—to do this job, you must be able pick up heavy luggage all day long and push wheelchairs around for fragile passengers. It's clear that your condition won't allow you to do that." Phil's reply? "If you don't let me try, you'll never know."

He got the job, learning ways to move heavy bags and push wheelchairs in spite of his disability. This choice turned out to be a good thing, because it was at the airport that he would meet his future wife, Mary Ann—also employed at the airport. By the way, after a few months, Phil earned the nickname of "Slick." He could load more bags a minute (twenty-two) than most of his full-bodied colleagues.

Phil cheerfully tackled many tough challenges on his journey to his definite major purpose—becoming a McDonald's restaurant owner. He was an "Andy Frain" usher at the ballpark, a security screener at the airport, a student in college where he earned degrees in accounting and aeronautical engineering, an owner and driver of an Indy pace car, and a stock market investor. Each time he embarked on a new challenge, he was initially told no. Each time, he turned it into a yes. Defeat was not in Phil's vocabulary, no matter how unlikely his success seemed to others.

By the time Phil celebrated his twenty-first birthday, his initial five-hundred-dollar investment in stock had grown to ten thousand dollars. He was still working as a skycap at O'Hare airport and studying for his college exams. Fred Turner, McDonald's CEO, would often come through his station as he traveled the world from his home office in nearby Oakbrook. The two got to know one another. One day, Turner turned to Phil and said, "You should think about making a career with us."

Phil waited until he got his master's degree to follow up, figuring he'd be ready then. The more he thought about owning a McDonald's restaurant, the more excited he got. The idea grew to be more than a wish. It became a burning desire. Then an expectation. So Phil began the process—he made an application for a store franchise, thinking the process would be a breeze. After all, he knew the company's CEO.

Alas, McDonald's had its rules. His first application was turned down. "No business experience. Not enough money in the bank." What did Phil do? He went out and got business experience doing sales and marketing as a partner in a small computer training company. He also continued to save his money. Every year or so, he would reapply. New barriers surfaced with each application.

In sum, Phil was rejected *five times*. It was time to pull out all the stops. Nothing was going to get in the way of his dream. He went to his father for advice. Mr. Fuentes put him in touch with an attorney who specialized in such applications and contracts.

Bingo, a face-to-face interview at last!

The interview started out well but, noticing Phil's physical limitations, the McDonald's executive grew tentative. "I think the challenge of operating a restaurant may be too much for you," he said.

"You'll never know if you don't give me a chance," replied the determined young man.

"We'll call you," he said.

Phil was accepted as a McDonald's owner-operator in 1989 and never looked back. He worked harder than ever and longer hours than ever. His dream had come true and he wasn't about to let it go. Today, in addition to all his accomplishments and honors, Phil and Mary Ann are bringing up a new generation of winners.

Their fifteen-year-old son is an Eagle Scout and their thirteen-year-old daughter a national cheerleading champion.

The Major Causes of Personal Failure

The major causes of failure were outlined by Napoleon Hill when he did his research. My own studies have shown that when Latinos fail, they do so for some of the reasons listed. Are there any you have struggled with or that have hampered you? If so, you're not alone. Many of the successful Latinos outlined in this book have experienced and overcome barriers such as these. If any of these causes are getting in your way, resolve to do something about them starting today.

1. A feeling that you are not worthy
2. No definite major purpose
3. Anger over having been discriminated against
4. Inadequate education
5. Lack of self-discipline
6. "The world owes me" mentality
7. Lack of ambition
8. Inability to recognize opportunity
9. Negative mental attitude
10. A "Get them before they get me" mentality
11. The desire to get something for nothing
12. A distrust of those outside the family
13. Discriminating against Anglos
14. Discriminating against any race
15. Discriminating against other religions
16. Lack of persistence and follow through
17. Unfavorable childhood influences
18. Failure to reach decisions quickly
19. Habitually breaking your word

20. Not owning up to your own mistakes
21. Taking advantage of employees
22. Taking advantage of anyone
23. Consistent ingratitude and lack of manners
24. Fear of poverty
25. Fear of riches
26. Fear of criticism or loss of love
27. Fear of ill health or old age
28. Fear of loss of liberty or death
29. Unwillingness to go the extra mile
30. Desire for revenge
31. Puffed ego and vanity
32. Lack of vision and imagination
33. Disloyalty
34. Failure to inspire teamwork
35. Failure to be part of a team
36. Overcaution
37. Lack of caution
38. Meddlesome curiosity
39. Propensity to gossip
40. Inability to listen well
41. Persistent procrastination
42. Unstable home life
43. Substance abuse
44. Placing too much importance on self
45. Fear of success

The list is long. It could be much longer. You could probably add to it by having seen how others you know have been defeated in their quest for success.

My biggest personal failure was not devoting enough time to my children when they were growing up. I was so caught up with my self-importance and thinking about my own success that I missed some of the most precious years of their lives. It took many years to make up for my omission and many family meetings to give them a chance to vent their feelings. All is well now; we are a close and happy family. Still, I wish I had been wiser.

Your Attitude Toward Defeat

Remember the *pobre, chaparro y feo* story about the construction worker who, when I asked how he was doing, replied, "poor, short, and ugly?" Sure, he was trying to be funny, but his humor revealed how he felt about himself: defeated.

Always be aware of what you say to others and especially what you say to yourself. Your words say much about your attitude. Never let them be words of defeat. Remember what Napoleon Hill said: "Defeat is not failure unless and until you accept it as such."

Creative Thinking
—Anna Cabral

Creative vision is found in confident people who are unafraid to try new things, in the few bold individuals not afraid to take a chance or to look beyond the horizon. It is present in those of you who are innovators and unafraid of criticism.

Christopher Columbus had the creative vision to sail uncharted waters to find a new world. La Reina Isabel had the creative vision to finance his voyage. Pablo Picasso had the creative vision to invent a whole new way of painting that created a revolution and earned him millions.

Napoleon Hill observes that creative vision belongs only to the people who go the extra mile, don't acknowledge eight-hour work days, and aren't focused on the almighty dollar. *Their aim is to do the impossible.*

Take a Dollar Out of Your Pocket

Look at a dollar bill closely. Chances are you will see the name and signature of Anna Cabral just below the seal of the U.S. Federal Reserve System. If her name isn't on your money, you may be holding a counterfeit bill. Or an old one. The Cabral name will be on every piece of printed U.S. currency for years. She is the treasurer of the United States. Her office oversees the White House front lawn and is filled with beautiful antiques that came from some of the most historic office buildings and homes in Washington. In my opinion, next to the Oval Office, she has the best one in the world.

Anna Cabral was born Anna Teresa Escobedo in San Bernardino, California, and couldn't speak English when she started the first grade. Her father was a farm worker, handyman, and jack-of-all-trades who worked harder than anybody. He lived to work. Throughout his life he frequently changed jobs, moving the family from city to city in search of a better payday. It was not unheard of to move his family from one side of town to the other if he thought it would improve their circumstances. The Escobedos seldom lived in one house for more than a few months. Each time he found a better job, they moved. If he lost his job, they moved. If he quit his job, they moved. The family never questioned it. They dutifully and happily made the best of each new adventure. No denying, el Señor Escobedo had gypsy in him.

Perhaps the nomadic lifestyle had an effect on young Anna. From the first grade to the third, her grades were rarely higher than Ds. She wasn't interested in school. Making good grades didn't seem important. In school she daydreamed, waiting for the last bell to ring. In the middle of her third year in school, her teacher, possibly frustrated with Anna's disinterest in class, remarked, "You're stupid. You don't even try!"

The eight-year-old was devastated. The words made her feel horrible. They also made her angry, angry enough to make a vow to herself. "I'll never let anyone say that to me again." Overnight, her attitude changed. Anna created a new vision for herself even at that young age. She began to pay attention in class. Suddenly, the impossible seemed possible. Ds became As. She began to put her full energy into her work that in turn attracted an encouraging response from her teachers. All at once, they realized that she was exceptionally smart.

"This attention is great," thought Anna. "I can get used to this." She'd never experienced praise at school before. Her newfound recognition triggered a total turnaround. From that day on, she became a star pupil. Even a superstar pupil. And there would be no turning back.

Anna's mother and father had both dropped out of school at an early age, a common practice among Latino working families at the time. Not finishing high school had been a barrier for them and they knew it. They wanted something better for their children. They thought a high school diploma would be the key. The Escobedos were determined to make it happen for Anna, her brother, and three sisters.

As the family grew, the moves from place to place and town to town continued. Palm Springs, Donner Lake, San Jose. Back to San Bernardino. Every so often, they would return to a familiar town or neighborhood. The kids loved it when this happened. It gave them a chance to hook up with old friends.

Both of Anna's parents worked long hours. Being the oldest, it became her job to take care of things at home. By age nine, Anna had developed into the co-parent to her younger siblings. There were three parents—Mom, Dad, and Anna.

One day, her father hurt his back at work. He was unable to walk or work. Then her mother got sick. She couldn't work. There was no income. The proud, hardworking family had to go on welfare, something they found unacceptable. For months, they lived on cornmeal, dry milk, cheese, butter, and bone chicken—staples provided by the department of agriculture for the needy. But this was no way to live, they thought.

After a few months, things started looking up. Dad got better. In school, Anna did so well that she was placed in a special class for gifted students. As soon as Señor Escobedo could walk, he bought an old pickup truck. The family went into the scrap metal business. They scoured the neighborhood for any discarded item that contained metal. They picked up washing machines, window air conditioners, old stoves and refrigerators, even soda pop and beer cans. When they found an old motor, the Escobedo children separated the plastic covering from the wiring so the clean metal could fetch top dollar.

At age sixteen, the ever-responsible Anna decided that she had to work full time because the scrap metal business wasn't bringing in enough income to support the family. She was a junior in high school but had earned enough credits to graduate because she had taken the right courses and consistently scored top grades. "I've reached my goal of getting my high school diploma," she reasoned. "Now it's time to start making money to help the family."

When she told Phillip Lamma, her favorite teacher, what she was doing, he got involved. Really involved. "You *must* go to college," he said. "You're one of the best students here and perfect college material. If you quit now to go to work, you'll solve a short-term financial problem but you'll cut off your future opportunities."

"College? I never even thought of college."

"Well, start thinking about it now."

"We don't have the money."

"I'll find the money."

"I can't leave home."

"It's not far—The University of California at Santa Cruz."

"I don't have a place to live."

"You'll live in the dorms."

"I can't afford room and board."

"We'll get that taken care of, too."

"But my family needs me."

"You'll help them more by getting an education. Let me talk to your parents."

Mr. Lamma spent hours convincing the Escobedos to allow Anna to go off to college. He then went a step further. He helped Anna fill out her applications for admission, financial aid, and housing. He pulled out all the stops—the sixteen-year-old Anna was getting enrolled in college, come hell or high water!

Phillip Lamma's hard work and faith in Anna's ability paid off. The young lady was admitted into California's tough university system—not as a freshman but as a sophomore! As an added bonus, the campus at Santa Cruz happened to be near her grandmother's house. *¡Que suerte!* "What luck!" She wasn't so far from home after all.

A New World Opens Up

As soon as Anna got to Santa Cruz, she was assigned to a work-study program run by Olivia Chavez, the director of the university's office of Education Opportunity Development. UC was making a big effort to recruit Latino students, particularly the children of migrant farmworkers. They formed the office to recruit them and to help mentor them once they arrived. The job was made to order for Anna. The kids could relate to her. She was as young or younger than many of them. She came from a poor working family. To top it off, she was having big success in college. She became the perfect tutor. The perfect mentor. And a wonderful role model.

Part of Anna's job was speaking at local high schools about college readiness and success. When she spoke, she saw the students' eyes light up as she told her story. She could almost hear them thinking, "If this kid from the barrio can do it, I can do it too!" *¡Si ella puede, yo también puedo!"*

After one of Anna's high school visits, one of the teachers came up to her and said, "I always thought these visits by college folks were a waste of time, but you've changed my mind. You speak to these kids in a way they understand. Keep up the good work."

Those words, coupled with the response she was getting from the students, convinced Anna that she could be an advocate and make a difference in the Latino community. She had a new mission—to advance the lives of young Latinos through better education. She joined most all the activist Chicano organizations on campus. She went to work like never before. She knew she could make a difference.

In her second semester, at one of the student rallies, Anna, now eighteen, met a tall, handsome law student by the name of Victor Cabral. He attended UC Davis, not far away. A bit older than Anna, he was wise, refined, and had a gentle way about him. They fell head over heels in love. Anna transferred to Davis to be close to Vic. They got married and looked forward to a bright future. They both wanted babies, and babies they had: four in just five years.

Anna became a wife, a mother, a student, a mentor, and a Chicano activist. Still, her role as a mother was her top priority. To tend to her family, she dropped out of school in her junior year. When the youngest of the four was out of diapers, she went back and finished. At age twenty-five, she got her degree.

By now Victor had set up a law practice and was attracting good business. Anna had her own degree and was weighing her options. She had begun to help manage the law firm and found it exciting and invigorating. "Why don't you apply to law school? We could both be lawyers and practice together," Victor suggested. The more they thought about it, the better it sounded.

Once again, creative vision and imagination came into play. The young couple decided to shoot for the stars. Anna would apply for a joint law degree at Berkeley School of Law at Boalt Hall and to the Kennedy School of Government at Harvard. To no one's surprise, she was accepted. After all, she had been an outstanding student throughout her college career. It wasn't just her smarts that earned her admission. It wasn't just her ability to think accurately with creative vision. It was also her daily application of several of the other seventeen principles outlined in this book. Anna always goes the extra mile. She has personal initiative. She controls her attention. She keeps a positive mental attitude and budgets her time and money remarkably well.

Creative Vision Goes Beyond Imagination

When counseling college students, I frequently ask them about their plans after they get their degree. Frequent answers are, "I don't know yet, I'm not sure," or, "All I care about is getting that diploma. I'll cross that bridge when I get to it." When I probe further, I find that there is usually a dream inside their head they have not shared. Or a fantasy they have not fully developed. In most cases, I discover that their imagination has been at work, but not always directed at a definite major purpose.

To fulfill your definite major purpose you need to go beyond what you can imagine. You need to harness your creative vision and put it to work. Creative vision, Napoleon Hill says, requires you to stimulate your imagination toward your goal and put the results of that imagination to work.

Some people stimulate their imagination in ways that don't further their definite major purpose. Take Anna's third-grade teacher and her insensitive comment. What if a teacher had said that to you? It could have set you off and sent your imagination in the wrong direction.

"She said I'm stupid."

"Am I stupid?"

"Maybe I *am* stupid."

"I must be stupid."

"What's the use?"

Many a young person would have given up right then and there. Had Anna's imagination swerved into the territory of inaccurate thinking, she could have been lost.

Another reaction to that comment might be:

"She doesn't like Mexicans."

"She's discriminating because I'm Latino."

"All Anglos are bad."

"I'll never trust them."

If you let your imagination go to dark places, it will create a world of negativity that has no correlation with reality. Maybe Anna's teacher had a headache that day. Maybe she was frustrated or tired. Maybe she just wanted to shock Anna into trying harder. Whatever sparked her ill-advised comment, we'll never know. We can just be thankful that the creative vision inside that little girl sparked a new beginning in her.

Your imagination is a wonderful thing. A powerful thing. You must be careful with it. It's like the wind and can blow you in any direction. It's your responsibility to harness its power to keep you moving toward your definite major purpose. You can do it. With accurate thinking, a positive mental attitude, and creative vision.

Anna Cabral always knew her definite major purpose had something to do with improving the lives of people, particularly Latinos. People with creative vision often pursue this type of goal. It fits Napoleon Hill's description of them: people who go the extra mile, recognize no nine-to-five working hours, and aren't concerned with monetary rewards. *Their aim is to do the impossible.*

This describes Anna Cabral perfectly. She kept doing the impossible. The Berkeley-Harvard joint degree program allowed her to choose between staying in California or moving across the country to Massachusetts. Staying in California would have been nice, but the courses offered at Harvard were what she was looking for. She and Victor made their decision; he sold the law firm, and off they went.

The young couple, with their four children, took their belongings and made the three-thousand-mile trek to Lexington, a small community fifteen miles from Harvard where the rent was cheaper. Instead of renting, however, they bought a house: a fixer-upper with a million things to repair. The plan was for Victor to work on the house while Anna went to school. The monthly income from the sale of the law firm would cover expenses.

Bad plan. Victor hated being a carpenter. The job was also much more than one person could handle. They had bitten off more than they could chew.

"What if we work on it together?" suggested Anna. "It'll be fun and we'll learn a lot in the process."

"Sounds like a plan," agreed Vic.

Together they not only fixed the house, they completely rebuilt it, adding a second story and making it beautiful and comfortable. It took them two years and countless hours of hammering, drywalling, and painting. They did it all themselves, from building new windows to replacing the roof tiles. All this while going to school and taking care of the four little Cabrals, one of whom was growing up faster than they expected.

Once again, the responsibilities of family interrupted. Anna deferred law school to oversee their children. By now, Victor and Anna had a $100,000 student-loan debt. The money from the sale of the firm dried up. To top it off, they were both unemployed.

It was time to put their creative vision to work once again. They looked around and sold their house at a profit just before the market went south. Victor secured a position in Washington, D.C., with the Department of Justice. Opportunities for Anna to fulfill her definite major purpose, however, seemed nonexistent. The only position she could find in Latino community outreach was with

Senator Orrin Hatch from Utah. The job sounded perfect. The situation did not. Hatch was a Republican! Anna was a staunch Democrat, and an active one at that.

"Go check it out," said Vic.

"What? And sell out? No way!"

"Give him a chance. He really wants to talk to you. This may be your chance to help the Latino cause."

As a courtesy to her husband and because no Democrat had such a position open, Anna reluctantly went for an interview with the senator.

Hatch made her a deal she couldn't refuse. "I need you to help me make a difference for Latinos in Utah," he said. "If you come work for me, I promise to always listen, to hear you out, to respect your opinions and recommendations, and to do my level best to implement them."

She took the job. The senator remained true to his word. He had the last say, of course, but Anna was his Latino conscience on the Hill for nine years. And a strong one at that. In Washington, she learned that in government nothing gets done without consensus. She learned to interact with members of Congress from both parties. She researched the issues and concerns of the community and helped the senator find solutions. Anna also learned that government is not always the answer. Sometimes it's the problem.

Anna used the skills she acquired on the senator's staff in her next career as president of HACER, the Hispanic Association for Corporate Responsibility. This is a coalition of the country's top Hispanic organizations. They use their combined clout to further Latino participation in corporate America. HACER made record progress under her leadership, adding dozens of Latinos to the boards of directors of Fortune 1000 companies.

After four years at HACER, Anna was recruited by the Smithsonian Institution to direct their Latino outreach. After only a year there Anna got a call from the president of the United States. "I need you," he said, asking her to serve as the treasurer of the United States, one of the most coveted positions in Washington. She was sworn into office in February 2005. As treasurer, she promotes the president's "Ownership Society" as well as his messages on tax reform, social security reform, homeland security, and financial literacy, an important Latino issue. In her travels she will work to improve the economic opportunities between the United States and Latin America.

Not bad for the daughter of a humble, hardworking California family, for a girl who didn't speak English when she entered the first grade. And not bad for the community she serves so very well.

Creative Vision Is Needed Today

Creative vision is needed today more than ever:

- In an ever smaller and interdependent world fraught with terror and fear of freedom lost, we need to find ways for people of diverse cultures, backgrounds, and religions to better understand, respect, trust, and care for one another.
- In an America that will soon find itself with no one demographic or cultural group as the majority, we must understand that no matter who we are, where we or our ancestors came from, or how long we've been in this country, our common goals unite us. That as Americans we all want the same thing—a better life for our children and the opportunity to fulfill the promise of the American Dream, based on our initiative and hard work.
- Creative vision is needed to help lift the spirits of those in our country who have lost their way and those who impose limitations on themselves.
- Creative vision is needed to raise the educational expectations of our young and their parents, particularly those who have never even thought of going to college.

Good Health
—Jeff Garcia

If your mind conceives an idea and your mind believes in that idea, your mind will allow you to achieve it. You know that by now. Knowledge of this truth has driven tens of thousands of people just like you toward amazing achievement. Now it's time to take this understanding a step further. To do that, we must now consider *the mind and the body as one unit.*

A healthy mind helps develop a healthy body. A healthy body fuels the work of a healthy mind. Each contributes to the other to form a perfect unit. Hill called it the mind-body. Your mind-body is one with nature. The two cannot be separated.

The Mind-Body Influence

Have you ever made yourself sick just thinking about something bad happening? Most of us have at one time or another. We can get a cold or the flu when we are heavily stressed at work. We develop headaches thinking about a bill we can't pay. Or a stiff neck and backache worrying about our next career move. That's the mind affecting the body. That's the mind-body at work.

When I was a recruit in a Marine Corps boot camp, our drill instructor made an announcement. The next day at the base swimming pool, each of us would jump from a forty-foot tower into water fifteen feet deep. "Everyone will jump," he barked, "including nonswimmers. You will learn to swim one way or another. Real Marines are swimmers!"

I was mortified. I couldn't swim a stroke. What if I drowned? To make matters worse, we had been taken to the pool the day before to observe other recruits going through the drill. The coaches had been especially insensitive to nonswimmers, forcing them to jump from the four-story platform, then leaving them to flail helplessly in the water until they almost passed out.

Just thinking of enduring that torture made me nauseated. That night, I couldn't sleep. The image of me fifteen feet underwater and not able to reach the surface dominated my thoughts and frightened me. When morning finally came, I threw up. As we lined up toward the tower, I threw up again, this time all over a fellow recruit and even into the pool. "Get that idiot out of here and over to sick bay." Those were the sweetest words I ever heard the drill instructor say. Interestingly, by the time I reached the nurse's station, my condition had cleared up.

Thankfully, I got through boot camp without ever having to make the jump. To this day, I'm convinced that my actions were quite conscious. My mind told my body what it had to do to keep from going into that pool!

Great Athletes and the Mind-Body

Great athletes work as hard developing their minds as they do developing their bodies. They know they will win only if their mind tells them they will win. Conversely, if their mind can't convince their body, in all likelihood they will lose no matter how perfectly conditioned their body may be. The same applies to you. In reading this book, you're getting your mind in shape to win at the game of life. As you do so, you will want to get your body in top shape, too. A strong, healthy body allows your mind to work at its best.

If you're an NFL football fan, you know the name Jeff Garcia. Jeff was the starting quarterback for the San Francisco 49ers for five years, where he broke records—even some set by the great Joe Montana.

Jeff Garcia is an athlete who understood the concept of the mind-body unit at an early age. As soon as Jeff could walk, his father, a junior college football coach, took him to the games to watch the play from the sidelines. He viewed the game from a player's point of view even as a small boy. Jeff observed and learned about football under his father's watchful eye. As he got older, he watched the older athletes working on their mind game as they got ready for the big game. When he got to high school, Jeff's father let him work out and practice after school with the junior college athletes even though they were bigger and stronger. Jeff learned to work harder, be faster, and play smarter than the more experienced players. He was always the little guy keeping up with the bigger ones.

Jeff's mother is Irish and his father Mexican. His skin is so fair and his hair so light that he looks 100 percent gringo. But don't let his looks deceive you. "I identify strongly as a Latino. My name is Garcia and I'm proud of my heritage," he says. "Our values teach hard work, dedication, responsibility, and family closeness. These are the values that guide my life."

Both sides of Jeff's family are from California and have agrarian roots. The Irish side were the farm owners. The Mexican side were the farmworkers. When his parents married, they settled in the small farm town of Gilroy, down the road from San Francisco and San Jose. Jeff had chores to do every morning before he left for school. He fed the horses and chickens and moved the heavy irrigation pipes into position for that day's watering. Every day he did his chores and behaved politely, meeting his parents' highest expectations.

Jeff felt that he had a responsibility to be a good son. When he was seven, his six-year-old brother drowned while on a family picnic. More grief followed. The next year, his five-year-old sister was killed when she fell out the back of a farm truck their father was driving. These tragedies were almost more than the family could bear, and instilled in young Jeff a sense of purpose. It would be his duty to make sure that his parents saw no more heartbreak. It would be up to him to make and keep them happy.

Losing his brother and sister taught Jeff that there are certain things he would never be able to control. He accepted that truth, but it made him aware that there are certain things he could control. His mind. His body. He would use them both to fulfill his newfound goal: to become an NFL quarterback, and to play for his favorite team, the San Francisco 49ers.

The Rhythms of Life

Jeff Garcia looks at physical conditioning and keeping fit as a natural rhythm of life. "You strengthen your body by eating the right food and doing the proper exercise. You strengthen your mind by making the right decisions and having the proper beliefs. It's all a matter of getting down to business," he says.

You can make *getting down to the business of total fitness* a natural rhythm in your own life if you decide to do so. If you work at making it a habit. If you don't let the idea of exercise overwhelm you by trying to do too much at one time. We all know you can't get from A to Z in a single step. It takes twenty-six. How many steps will it take to get your body into top-notch condition? That depends on its condition today. If you're in relatively good shape and not overweight, it may take six months. If you've been a couch potato for some time, it may take a year or two, even three. But that's okay. No matter where you are, to get to where you want to be, *all you need to do is to begin.*

Jeff's winning strategy is to take it one step at a time. At the beginning of each game he says, "I will be the best quarterback *on this field on this day.*" At that moment, he doesn't care about being the most valuable player in the Super Bowl. All that matters is that he is the best quarterback on that field and the best quarterback on that field on that day.

If he accomplishes those two short-term goals every time he plays, he will most likely lead his team to a win. If his team wins often enough, it will most likely get in the playoffs. If it gets into the playoffs often enough, it will most likely go to a Super Bowl.

If you apply Jeff's philosophy to body conditioning, all you have to do is the best workout you can *wherever you are* and the best workout you can on *that day.*

Applying Jeff's approach to improving your body gives you permission to focus only on what you can do and will do each day. Here's a technique that helps me: when I go to bed each night, I think about looking forward to doing my exercise first thing the next morning. As I'm dozing off I tell myself, "When I wake up in the morning, I will be refreshed, looking forward to a good workout. I will do it before showering and before breakfast."

When you get up in the morning, go to the bathroom, brush your teeth, and comb your hair. But don't do anything else unless it's turning on a good exercise video or the page to your favorite exercise book. Which routine should you choose? It doesn't really matter. Go to the bookstore or to Amazon and pick whatever suits you best. Order a Bowflex if you want. The key is to do *something* every day (or every other day if that's what your program recommends) and do it to the best of your ability.

Some people prefer to stay in shape by walking an hour a day. They find this regular exercise invigorates them, releases tension and stress, and gives them energy to perform at their best. Others may prefer to prepare for and run a marathon. Still others opt for the rigors of an Iron Man competition. Whatever workout choice you make, just make sure you make it. A healthy mind depends on a healthy body.

The Force of a Positive Mental Attitude

By most accounts, Jeff Garcia wasn't professional football material. He's too small. NFL scouts look for college quarterbacks taller than six feet three inches and who weigh somewhere between 220 and 240 pounds. As a college senior, Jeff was six feet tall and weighed 160 pounds.

His smaller size had never been a problem as far as Jeff was concerned. Remember, he always played with the big kids. His college career was stellar. In his first game as a starter at San Jose State, he threw five touchdown passes against UNLV to win the game. As a senior, he made the East-West Shrine Team. In his last game, his West team was trailing 28-to-7 when Jeff was sent in. He saved the day, throwing for three touchdowns and making a two-point conversion at the minute to beat the East 29-to-28. His whole family was there to watch. What a way to end the season!

Jeff started his college football career with a bang, performed consistently, and finished at the top of the stats, but got no NFL offers. It seemed the NFL scouts were more interested in the height and weight of a player, and less interested in how well he played.

Jeff knew he could do the job and didn't give up. He kept the faith and stayed in top physical condition waiting for the call.

He got it.

But not from the NFL. The Calgary Stampeders in the Canadian Football League took a chance the NFL wouldn't. They made Jeff Garcia their quarterback. Their decision paid off when Jeff took the team to the Grey Cup Championship!

Garcia began to settle in and feel comfortable in his new Canadian community. Things were going beautifully. He was a local hero, and his team was at the top of its game. "Looks like the NFL is not going to happen. Might as well start living my life here," he thought. He opened Garcia's Mexican Restaurant as a way to settle in and as a way to keep his favorite Mexican food available in Calgary.

When the NFL noticed the great and consistent job Garcia was doing in Canada, they gave him another look. Now the Oakland Raiders, Miami Dolphins, St. Louis Rams, Jacksonville Jaguars, and San Francisco 49ers were all interested. He got firm offers from Miami and San Francisco. Jeff, of course, signed on with San Francisco, the team that he had worshiped as a kid.

In San Francisco, Jeff had big shoes to fill. Joe Montana and Steve Young were still the big heroes there, and their records as 49er quarterbacks were legendary. Still, Jeff broke several of them. He was a Pro Bowl quarterback three years in a row. He was the first 49er to throw for thirty-eight touchdowns in back-to-back seasons, and he was first to complete three hundred passes in three consecutive seasons.

Jeff Garcia was the smaller guy. He was the shorter guy. Yet, because he performed, he earned the respect and admiration of football fans and players throughout America. He showed that he belonged in the NFL. What he lacked in size, he made up in hard work, study, and conditioning. As I write this, Jeff is in his twelfth season as a professional football player. At age thirty-five, he enjoys the game as much as ever. "I'm working out today as hard as I did when I was twenty-one. I will work as hard as I need to work to stay in competitive condition."

In many ways, Jeff is lucky. He had his dad as his coach. He had early exposure to older, more experienced players who challenged him. He had the support of his family and friends who encouraged him. All that, however, didn't guarantee success. Jeff's success came because he applied several of the principles of personal achievement:

1. He had a goal to be an NFL quarterback.
2. He had faith in his goal and applied it.
3. He goes the extra mile.
4. He keeps a positive mental attitude.
5. He enforces self-discipline.
6. He inspires teamwork.
7. He understands the importance of the mind-body unit.
8. He maintains sound health by getting down to the business of working out every day to keep his body in the same finely tuned condition as his mind.

Effective Mind-Body Stimulants

Napoleon Hill was among the first to write about the importance of the mind and its effect on the body. In his research, he discovered twelve essential mental stimulants that boost the health of both. I've added a few of my own.

1. *Family.* The unit that makes life complete, especially for Latinos. Helping one another and being there for each other is a wonderful stimulant.
2. *Children.* Life's greatest joy! In them you see the future as well as a better version of yourself. In teaching them to be good, you remind yourself to be better. In teaching them new things and showing them new places, you make new discoveries.
3. *Love.* The ultimate expression of positive energy and emo-

tion. This unleashes all the creative forces that advance human destiny.

4. *Sex.* A completely natural desire. It is an expression of love, intimacy, and trust. You must never misuse it either by being unfaithful or by getting addicted to it. Being unfaithful can ruin your family life and stagnate your career. Addiction to sexual stimulation will misdirect your energy. Don't get tempted by unwanted e-mails from scuzzy sites. Sex is a great stimulant. It has inspired both men and women to do great things. It is also a wonderful way to relieve stress and gain tranquility.

5. *Friendship.* Couldn't do without it. We learn together, play together, and share our most intimate secrets with friends.

6. *Mastermind alliances.* The people who are on the journey to success with you will stimulate your imagination and increase your determination to do great things. They will help get you through the tough times, too.

7. *Desire.* Fans and stimulates your energy and drive.

8. *Work.* Properly and efficiently directed, it is the heart of productivity.

9. *Exercise.* Drives away frustration, releases pent-up stress, and stimulates the brain with increased blood and oxygen.

10. *Sleep.* Refuels the body and relaxes your mind.

11. *Play.* Lets the conscious mind rest and the subconscious go to work.

12. *Breathing.* Drawing air deep into your lungs and stomach relaxes you and increases brain function.

13. *Music.* Can relax, stimulate, and inspire the mind, body, and soul.

14. *Water.* Eight glasses a day keeps the doctor away. Lack of water drains your energy and weakens your immune system.

15. *Autosuggestion.* Talking to your subconscious, especially as you're falling asleep, is a wonderful way to dig up new ideas and to solve problems.

16. *Faith and religion.* The noblest of all stimulants, these are often
the most effective.

Always remember to keep your mind-body unit in sync. If you
overwork your mind and not your body, you may die a young genius. If you overwork the body and not the mind, you will never
know your true potential.

Budgeting Time and Money
—Joe Reyes

Men and women who are successful in achieving their definite major purpose make the most of every dollar. And the most of every hour. They waste neither time nor money. You will notice that truly successful people are rarely rushed. They are calm. They don't overschedule their time or insert frivolous meetings on their calendar. They know what items to put on it and what items to leave off. They make entries for family time. They make entries for vacations and relaxation. They make entries for helping people and serving their community. What's the key thought here? Don't put anything on your calendar that doesn't take you closer to your goal.

When budgeting their money, they have a sense of balance. They are not afraid of spending. But they don't throw their money away. They don't spend more than they have or borrow more than they can repay. They make smart choices. Many delight in taking smart risks. When they do take risks, they take only those that will help them reach their definite major purpose.

How good are you at managing your time and money? Let's

decide by using a combination of Napoleon Hill's and my check-lists. Use it the way pilots do before every flight. Ask yourself these questions every day:

1. Do I spend at least thirty minutes each day using my imagination and creative vision toward the realization of my major definite purpose?
2. Do I fan the flames of my burning desire every single day?
3. Each day, do I take at least one step to do at least one thing that gets me closer to my definite goal?
4. Do I spend a predetermined amount of time each week brainstorming with my mastermind alliance?
5. When I suffer a temporary setback, do I make time to fully analyze what I have learned from my mistake and use it as a chance to improve?
6. Do I spend my time really planning or merely dreaming or (even worse) complaining about what went wrong?
7. How often do I disregard my plans and change them in midstream, substituting personal pleasure for work or the other way around?
8. Do I use every moment of time as if it were the only one I had?
9. Do I regard each moment as an opportunity to change the course of my life for the better?
10. Is my mental attitude as positive as it can be each day? Do I have frequent lapses into negative thinking?
11. Do I display personal initiative each day?
12. Did I go the extra mile today?
13. Did I read an article or a book, or did I follow the example of someone I admire to further my journey toward my definite major purpose this week?
14. Did I reread my definite major goal six times today?
15. Did I display the attributes of a pleasing personality throughout the day?

16. Did I apply my faith today? Am I a true believer in my definite major purpose?

17. Did I control my self-discipline today or did I let my uncontrolled emotions take me off course?

18. Am I replacing my fears with ambition and positive thoughts?

19. Am I ridding myself of the barriers that bring about the negative or inaccurate thinking of generations past?

20. Did I inspire cooperation today by my thoughts and actions?

21. What problems did I solve today? How did I enlist the help of my mastermind alliance or team to solve them?

22. Did I exercise today?

23. Did I spend at least an hour of quality time with my family today?

24. Did I spend at least eight hours of quality time with my family this weekend?

25. Did I tell each member of my family I love them today?

This last one takes one second to say it and it reaps amazing rewards.

Don't Give Up One to Have the Other

Some people believe that to achieve wealth or success, you must sacrifice time with your family. That's true only if you believe it. Remember, your mind will give you whatever you tell it. If you tell it, "To achieve my goal, I will have to give up my family life," then it will give you your goal but at the expense of your family. If you tell it, "To achieve my goal, I will have to give up my weekends or my vacations," then your days will be all work and no play. That's not good for your body. Or your soul.

To achieve a good balance of work, family, community, and leisure, all you have to do is deal with every appointment equally. Treat your family time as appointments on your calendar in the same way you do a business appointment. Don't remove a family appointment because a client or boss called. Your child's soccer game is every bit as important as anything else. The next story is a perfect example.

The founder of the largest Latino-owned business in the United States found the time to do everything he ever wanted. He found the time to help raise seven boys and one daughter. He found the time to educate them. He found the time to train them to be his business partners and to help run the family businesses. He found the time to keep the flame of love burning with Frannie, his wife of fifty years. He finds time to spend with his twenty-one grandchildren. He finds the time to travel and serve his community and church. He finds the time to exercise each day.

And Joe Reyes exercises hard. At seventy-eight, he looks as young and as strong as Arnold Schwarzenegger. Joe always has a smile on his face and a kind word for everyone. To me, he's a Latino Ronald Reagan with pumping iron muscles. He does three hundred crunches a day. Joe is a very low-key guy. He shies away from publicity. Throughout his career, he's stayed out of the limelight but never out of the work site. The company he founded evolved into today's Reyes Holdings LLC, which is run by several of his sons. It ranks seventeenth among the largest privately held companies in the United States.

The dapper Mr. Reyes always looks ready for his close-up. His shoes are spit-shined. His suits are tailor-made. His beautiful white-on-white Irish linen shirts sparkle. His silk ties are as flamboyant as they are tasteful. His ever-present bright breast-pocket handkerchief is artfully exposed two inches. I forgot to mention—Joe finds the time to dress, as well.

Joe Reyes calls himself "a true Mexican and a true peddler," although he wasn't born in Mexico and no one else would call him a peddler. He believes that being a peddler is the highest form of humanity. Maybe he's right. Joe has made a nice living selling everything from beer to bridges to burger meat to cardboard boxes. This is how *Forbes* magazine describes the company he founded:

> Closely held Reyes Holdings has a grip on two things that are complementary—food and beer. Through its subsidiaries Reyes Holdings distributes products throughout North, Central, and South America. One of these, the Martin-Brower Company, supplies McDonald's restaurants in the US and Canada, as well as serving Brazil, Central America, and Puerto Rico.
>
> Reyes Holdings also owns Premium Distributors of Virginia, Chicago Beverage Systems, and California's Harbor Distributing among the beer wholesalers it owns. Reyes operates distribution centers in the US and six other countries. Co-chairmen Chris Reyes and Jude Reyes and VP David Reyes (Joe's sons) own the firm.

Recently, the Reyes brothers acquired Reinhart, the nation's third largest independent food service distributor. We have to agree, that's a lot of peddling.

How did Joe, the founder of this empire, do it all? By, he says:

1. Being fearless
2. Being confident
3. Listening well
4. "Giving never up" (more on that later)
5. Learning to leverage borrowed money
6. Keeping his eyes open to opportunities
7. Making and keeping many friends
8. Making sure everybody wins
9. Managing time

10. Managing money
11. Being damn lucky

Learning to Be Fearless and Confident

Joe learned fearlessness and confidence as a Navy fighter pilot in the Korean War flying F4Us. By the time the war was over, he had been on two hundred strikes, earning him the distinction of a Double Centurion on the line. He looked death in the face many times. On occasion, flying back to the carrier after a strike, the night would be pitch black. Somewhere in that blackness was his carrier's tiny landing strip. When he got lucky, lightning from a storm would light the way. Happy to find the carrier, Joe would come in for the approach. The wrath of these storms would pitch the huge ship from side to side, up and down, and front to back. With water coming down in sheets and the wind blowing his small one-man fighter plane off the landing path, he made many a harrowing landing.

"The tough part wasn't the landing," says Joe, "it was the enemy ground fire I had to dodge." Of the original graduating class of forty-seven pilots, only thirteen were left standing at tour's end. One of them was Joe.

He never got hit.

He admits that during each mission, he felt the hand of the Lord guiding his plane. After surviving all those close calls, Joe felt he had nothing to fear. His confidence grew. "Now I can face anything," he said to himself.

Learning to Seize Opportunity

After his stint in the Navy, Joe Reyes came back to America to marry the love of his life and the most beautiful girl in the world, Frannie Collins. He earned a degree in electrical engineering from the University of Maryland and put it to work right away, securing a position at the Westinghouse Corporation to develop radar systems and to work on classified operations. After six successful years there, he left to start his own consulting firm representing companies that wanted to do business with the U.S. government. He landed contracts for his clients with the Department of Defense, the Department of Transportation, and others. He was signing up business left and right and loving it. His love of "peddling" was born.

One of the companies he was representing got a new CEO. "Don't make a move without clearing it with me," the CEO told him. "I'll tell you who to call on and what to say."

Joe didn't exactly cotton to that approach. He knew immediately that the chemistry wasn't right, promptly resigned, and took another route. He called on the presidents of the five divisions under that CEO to tell them what had happened. Four of them hired Joe on the spot and kept him on. "We need you, Joe. Just keep bringing in the business." Joe grew his business and kept his freedom.

He continued to develop new relationships and opportunities. He began representing bigger and bigger companies. One was Mason and Hanger, a major construction firm founded in 1827. It had built the Hoover Dam, the Pennsylvania Turnpike, and the Golden Gate Bridge, as well as military bases, roads, and major bridges all over the world. Joe made the firm even bigger by securing hundreds of millions of dollars in major government contracts. By now, he had refined his art: *using his time to focus only on the big picture—and the big opportunity.*

Give Never Up

The first words out of Joe Reyes's mouth when I sat down to interview him at the University Club in Washington, D.C., were, "Tell your reader to do four things: Listen. Look for opportunity. Give never up. Learn from their mistakes and temporary setbacks; let them become a challenge to propel you to greater things."

"You mean, never give up, right?"

"I mean, give never up. Think about it. You'll start to like it," Joe replied with a little gleam in his eye. I was still confused.

It was only after a chat with my smarter and better half, Kathy, that Joe's wisdom sunk in.

"Sure, I get it," she said. "It's like that boxer used to say, 'Impossible is nothing.' It's a way of turning words inside out to make you take a second look. If you give up the word 'never,' you give never up. Impossible is a negative word. It's best not to use it. Never is definitely negative. It's best not to use it, either. I think I'll give never up!"

Joe looks at things from a different angle. Most successful people love to give advice. Joe prefers to listen. "Listen and look for opportunity, look for opportunity, look for opportunity." It was then I understood. Joe Reyes is short on advice and long on example.

Joe's father was an entrepreneur. He led by example, too. He started out working in the oil fields of Ranger, Texas. He married and settled in San Antonio where he and a friend became grocery salesmen to mom-and-pop shops during the Great Depression. Times were tough. They struggled for several years and finally had to close shop. He started a candle company to sell *velitas* to religious Mexican families, but the families were too poor to buy. He went out of business a second time. He came back and started a bigger grocery distributing company but had to shut down when he let too many customers have too big a credit line. Still, the older Mr. Reyes came back again and again. He never gave up. Or better said, "he gave never up." He always earned enough to provide for the family. Years later, the older Mr. Reyes became a successful representative on one of Joe's contracts in Dilly, Texas. The old man had a great time working for his son. Joe learned a big lesson from his dad's resiliency. To give never up.

Making Friends and Managing Money

When Reyes was a young engineer working for Westinghouse, he earned about seven thousand dollars a year—not a bad paycheck in those days. A good and trusted friend, a Georgetown graduate, came to him with a great opportunity: to design, develop, and build a beautiful townhouse community in Maryland close to Washington, D.C. "All I need is a hundred and fifty thousand to make it happen," he said. Joe looked over the proposal and was convinced it would be successful.

"Where will you get the money?" Joe asked.

"Make me a loan."

"Are you crazy? I don't have that kind of money!"

"Well then, raise it for me."

"Raise it yourself."

"You're the salesman, I'm not. You can do it, I can show you how."

"How?"

"See all those older engineers who work with you? I'll bet every one of them has a nest egg of at least ten thousand. They're only earning 4 percent at the bank. Tell them you'll pay them 12½ percent interest a year and return their money in five years. If they don't buy, offer to return it in three years. You do that and I'll make you a partner. Deal?"

"Deal."

To Joe's amazement, all his colleagues wanted in. Their friends wanted in. They liked Joe and trusted him. They had witnessed him perform. He was their friend. Joe and his Georgetown buddy built the condos, sold them quickly, and earned a fair profit. The investors got their money back earning three times more than they would have at a bank. Everybody was a winner! Fifty years later, the condos still stand. They remain one of the area's beauty spots.

From this experience, Reyes learned two things: the value of friends and the value of money. "The more friends you have and the better you listen to them, the more opportunities will come your way. Friends tell their friends about you. It's exponential opportunity. That's how I raised the hundred and fifty thousand," says Joe.

He also learned the value of managing his money by using other people's money. "There's no debtor's prison," he says. He's right. They don't put you in jail for borrowing. Banks borrow all the time from the people who save with them. That's how they make their money.

Just like a bank, Joe borrowed. Just like a bank, he made a profit. Just like a bank, he made a profit for his lenders. He learned to make things happen even when he didn't have the money himself.

There are many lessons to be learned from the reserved and publicity-shy Señor Joseph A. Reyes. And the main one is this: *If you budget your time and money according to the way you see your goals and opportunities, you'll grow as rich as you want.* I'm not talking about just getting money rich. I mean getting heart, soul, and spirit rich.

18

The Cosmic Habitforce
—Virgilio Elizondo

Napoleon Hill's seventeenth and final principle, "the cosmic habitforce," is the icing on the cake. It gives your ability to "think & grow rich" a sense of wholeness and spirituality. This lesson can best be interpreted for Latinos by the respected theologian Father Virgilio Elizondo.

Let me tell you a bit about Virgil. In 2000, *Time* magazine named him "one of the spiritual leaders for the new millennium"— that's the next one thousand years! In the same issue, they named Martin Luther King Jr. and Gandhi as having been leaders for the past millennium. When the World Council of Churches produced an audio CD depicting the last hours of Christ on earth, they chose to use the voices of Father Elizondo and the Reverend Billy Graham, among others. This man walks in great company. And by knowing him, so do I.

My wife Kathy and I get together for dinner with our friend Virgilio once every three weeks or so. We partake of Kathy's marvelous cooking and drink the fine wines she picks. And we talk. Many times late into the night. Kathy and Virgilio are intellectuals. They come up with great themes, observations, and insights. I am the proverbial fly on the wall. Though far from silent, I mostly observe. Learn. And record.

As I think back, so many of our conversations, in some form or other, have had to do with this law of cosmic habitforce. This is the law that says that *every living creature, every particle of matter, is subject to the influence of its environment.* Said another way, it is the law that recognizes that you and your habits are influenced by the environment around you.

A person who grows up around drugs, poverty, unhappiness, and crime is more likely than others to form habits that will lead to failure and pain. Conversely, a person who grows up in a loving, stimulating, and positive environment is likely to form habits of success.

Only a small fraction of people in the industrialized world overcome negative surroundings and go on to accomplish great things. Another few vastly improve their already comfortable surroundings. Whether you grew up poor and impoverished or middle-class and comfortable, you are among those who will improve on what has been handed you. That's why you're reading this book.

Napoleon Hill explains the cosmic habitforce in these words: "The grandest example of cosmic habitforce is the operation of the heavens. Stars and planets move with clock-like precision. They don't collide. They don't suddenly veer off course. Attraction and repulsion keeps them moving so precisely, that for thousands of years, human beings have been able to predict the position of stars and planets, the timing of eclipses, and the regularity of meteor showers."

The universal order is reflected in Hill's statement. You don't control it. An infinite power does. What you can control are your actions and your habits. You become who you are because of them. Your repeated actions become your habits. Good or bad, your habits become you. But you can change, you can convert, you can retool yourself. Of course, you must *choose* to do it, and like any good athlete or artist, creating new habits will take diligence and determination.

Making *Limonada* Out of *Limones*

Father Virgilio's life story and his experiences illustrate this point. He likes to talk about the exceptional people he knows. The ones who learned to overcome the influences of their environment by virtue of their strong and positive habit patterns. These cases are noteworthy because they are so exceptional. We can learn much from them.

Virgilio tells the story of one of his parishioners, a young man in his early twenties by the name of Gerardo Olaz. Gerardo made his way to San Antonio from Costa Rica in pursuit of economic opportunity. He was an agile, all-around athlete and a terrific soccer player who dreamed of turning pro. When he got settled in the United States, he was hired on with a tree-trimming company and learned to operate heavy equipment. He was given responsibility and tough assignments. He worked long hours and never complained. By repeating positive thoughts, he developed a habit of optimism.

On Sundays, he would visit with Virgilio after mass and talked excitedly of his good fortune. He was saving money and sending it back to his mother in Costa Rica. Once he helped his mother get out of debt, he would return to his homeland to pursue his dream of a professional sports career.

One day, as he was trimming limbs off a high tree, he accidentally touched a live high-power line. In an instant, twenty-thousand volts of electricity tore through his perfect body, frying his hands where the bolt entered and his feet where it exited. He fell fifteen feet to the ground. "He's dead," they thought. "His insides are cooked." In virtually all cases when voltage this strong passes through the body, it sears a person head to toe.

"Wait! He's breathing," someone noticed. "Call an ambulance!" To this day, no one knows how Gerardo's internal organs survived the trauma. In this case, the surge of power fried his feet off and nearly destroyed his hands as well. The doctors at Brooke Army Medical Center tried a rare procedure in an effort to save his hands. They cut open his thighs and inserted his hands in them for several weeks to give them natural nourishment.

His recovery was long, slow, and painful. Father Elizondo took him in at the San Fernando Cathedral when the hospital released him. There, he and parish volunteers provided food and shelter while he healed. As the months passed, he learned to move his stiff fingers and to hold a fork once again. At Sunday masses, the congregation, at Virgilio's suggestion, collected money to fit Gerardo with a set of prosthetic feet.

It didn't take long for Gerardo to come to grips with the obvious; he would never be a professional soccer player. Still, he saw himself as a whole person. He did not complain about the accident, but thanked God for the miracle that saved his life and the many friends who helped him recuperate. Throughout his ordeal, his inner sense of optimism prevailed. He knew he could not control the cosmic habitforce. But he could, and did, control his own habitforce. When he was able, he returned to Costa Rica, where he soon married.

The last time Virgilio heard from him, he had a family and was working and teaching kids soccer. Gerardo had established optimistic habit patterns early in his life, so when tragedy struck he called on those habits to help him recover. From time to time, he grew depressed—as anyone in his situation surely would—but he refused to dwell on the things he could no longer do. He focused on what he could do. And he could do a lot.

Father Elizondo reflects, "What I have encountered in people like Gerardo, who have triumphed over mishaps and disasters, is their sense of gratitude for being alive and remarkable lack of jealousy toward others who are doing well. This gives them a great sense of inner freedom, peace, tranquility, and creative strength. They are not merely survivors, but incredible achievers."

You Are What You Do

As Napoleon Hill says, "Habits become part of your nature by repetition. If you create thought habits by repeating certain ideas in your mind, cosmic habitforce will take over these patterns of thought. You will make them more or less permanent in your mind, depending on your practice of repetition. The same thing will happen to physical practice."

People who exercise every day *look forward to exercising every day.* They tend to stay fit and healthy. People who watch TV all day *look forward to watching TV all day.* They tend to get fat and unhealthy. Be keenly aware of what you are thinking about most of the time. Know what your predominant thoughts and actions are. Thoughts become actions. Actions with repetition become habits. Habits become you.

Dichos, "Old Sayings"

There is a *dicho* that Father Virgilio believes describes the attitude of people who rise above the sometimes-destructive forces of life. "Some people see a beautiful rose and lament the fact that it has thorns; others see the ugly thorns and marvel at the precious rose that emerges from them." People who zero in on the filth, see filth. Those who prefer to see the beauty, see beauty. Those who triumph over disaster are those who have formed the habit of seeing the beautiful side of things.

The amazing thing is that the mind takes whatever thoughts you feed it by repetition and makes them real! Most all pessimists are unhappy, grumpy, and unsuccessful people. Optimists are both happy and successful. Which would you rather be? Remember, *whatever your mind conceives and believes you will achieve.* Will you achieve the rose? Will you achieve the thorn? Either is equally possible. It's all up to you. And your thoughts.

Now, put your book down. Take a few minutes to review your predominant thoughts for the last week. Write them down. Examine them closely. How many are of success? How many of them are of doubt and fear? By now, most of your thoughts should be thoughts of success. If they are, you are on your way to riches.

But wait! Do thoughts of poverty and obstacles still creep into your consciousness every now and then? If they do (and they will on occasion, especially if they have been your dominant thoughts for a while), replace them consciously with Napoleon Hill's art of autosuggestion. Pull out the piece of paper on which you've written down your goal. Read it again, and again. And again. As many times as it takes to replace thoughts of doubt and fear. In time, four to six weeks, optimistic thoughts of success will prevail. You will have won the battle.

Latinos Are Natural Optimists

No hay mal que por bien no venga is one of the best known of the Latino *dichos.* It means, "Good always comes from the bad stuff that happens." To Father Virgil, this saying sums up the Latino attitude toward life. This optimistic, relentless attitude combined with our deep faith in our God, our infinite intelligence and wisdom, makes us especially good candidates for the *pursuit* of success. Yet we must learn to turn these attributes into the *achievement* of success. He warns that the way we interpret our faith in God makes all the difference. Some see it as an escape from responsibility; others see it as a creative energy within us.

Latinos very often refer to God in very familiar terms. Father Elizondo advises us to internalize these phrases as a belief in infinite intelligence but never as blind dependence on it. *Lo que Dios quiera,* "Whatever God wants." *Como Dios quiera,* "However God wants." *Sea por Dios.* "It's the will of God." *Believing* in God should not translate into depending on God. This is because we share His infinite intelligence. Infinite intelligence and you are one and the same. After all, even the Bible says we were created in the image and likeness of a creative God, a god of infinite intelligence.

Father Virgilio says,

When people believe it's better to leave everything to the higher power, they become imprisoned by their own faith. They sit back and wait for infinite intelligence to make their decisions. They stop trusting their own instincts. They feel their instincts are separate from infinite intelligence. This is not so.

The best approach to decision making is to combine your faith in God with faith in yourself. You don't have to be a genius to be in touch with infinite intelligence. It's in you already. It is part of you. When you suffer a setback, it is not a 'punishment from God.' It is a learning experience from which you can emerge stronger and smarter. There is no such thing as absolute failure, just opportunity for new beginnings.

Father Elizondo is a wise and highly educated man. He earned a doctorate in Paris. He is the author of more than a dozen books, each of which has been translated into eight languages. He has lectured all over the world. Yet his learning comes as much from his parents who didn't finish grade school as it does from the halls of academia.

> As far as I can remember, my parents never doubted that I would go to college and that I would earn my degree. The alternative was never an option. How they came to that conclusion, I confess, I do not know. But they implanted the thought so deeply in my mind that I never questioned it.

Virgilio's dad, Don Virgil, was an entrepreneur. He came from Mexico at the start of the revolution, about 1911. He was a teen when he traveled alone to the United States to join a distant uncle in the grocery business. His uncle's grandfather had stayed in Texas after it had been ceded by Mexico some fifty years earlier. The two set up shop and called it Elizondo Grocery. Under their confident management style, it would thrive for decades.

Even as a young man, Don Virgil was adept at earning and saving money. He would always work for himself, not necessarily to be a millionaire, but to feel a sense of self-accomplishment. When the Lord called him, Mrs. Elizondo was left with their home and business fully paid for. He owed not a cent to anyone. He was not a wealthy man, but he fulfilled his wish—to establish a small business where he was his own boss.

What do these stories prove? First, that Latinos possess natural strengths. We love work. Hard work doesn't scare us. It invigorates us. We are natural optimists. We look at the bright side of things.

In recalling his childhood, Virgil tells of his parents taking responsibility and initiative at every turn. "Mom and Dad weren't 'churchy' people, but they had a deep sense of the supportive presence of a God who cared for them," he explains. "It is they who taught me that infinite power resides in every one of us. That belief gave them a sense of confidence. And the feeling of commitment to 'go for it' when they saw opportunity."

The Power of Collaborative Friendships

Don Virgil Elizondo believed in "collaborative friendships." Not just the guys getting together for a drink, but friends gathering to talk over possibilities and opportunities. Whenever he and his buddies got together, they went home having created something of value beyond good conversation. They talked about history and how it impacted their future. They talked about politics and how they could contribute. They talked about family and how they could help.

One member of the group was Peter Reed. They observed during one of those conversations that a lot of people in the neighborhood wanted to buy religious candles but couldn't find them. They wanted candles like the ones they could buy in Mexico, ones with images of La Virgen de Nuestra Señora de Guadalupe or of the patron saint of San Juan.

"There's a demand for *candelas religiosas*. One of us should go into the business of making them," Don Virgil observed. "I can do it," Reed said. He did and so the Reed Candle Co. was born. It was so successful that it made Peter Reed a millionaire, and when he died, he left his business to his two sons, Peter and Henry, who grew it into one of the biggest religious candle companies in the nation. They too became millionaires, all because of Virgil Elizondo's collaborative friendship started so many years before.

Today, business books would call those gatherings networking. Call it what you will; when a group of like-minded people get together to talk about opportunities and possibilities, great ideas are conceived. These great ideas can lead to a new way of looking at reality. Remember Hill's mantra, *whatever your mind can conceive and believe, you can achieve.*

The Educational Pact

The fathers in the "Elizondo group" often talked about improving future opportunities for their children. They wisely concluded that a college education would be the door-opener. They made a pact to make sure that their sons got college degrees. To understand how remarkable this pledge was, we need only remember that this was the early 1940s and almost no Latino family in the United States considered college for their boys. The girls? Forget it!

From the moment the group of men made their pact, Father Virgilio's educational future was sealed. He would be sent to a private military school. There he became friends with Anglos as well as with wealthy Mexicans. That experience taught him to feel comfortable with people different from himself. It also taught him to feel equal, to exercise his mind, and to believe that anything was possible.

From the elite Peacock Military Academy, it was on to the small, private Catholic St. Mary's University, where he earned a bachelor of science degree. This was a first-class education for someone from west San Antonio. At St. Mary's, his professors introduced him to the possibility of the priesthood. It would be his calling, his life's work. He went on to the seminary for four more years of advanced theological study. After ordination, he settled down to be the very best parish priest he could be.

But Virgilio Elizondo was destined to become much, much more. He was fascinated with the often-ignored Catholic teachings regarding the need for the church to be involved in all aspects of human rights and development. Never one to closely follow the church's traditional approach to doctrine, he became a radical of sorts. He took up the cause of civil rights, marched with César Chavez, supported Martin Luther King Jr., and demonstrated at city hall. He became a champion for the poor and the disparaged, undocumented workers. Virgilio understood their needs as well as their potential. To improve understanding and trust between cultures, he founded the now-famous Mexican American Cultural Center (MACC). The center attracts people from all over the world, teaching *Mestisaje,* or "the benefits of mixing races, cultures, and languages in everyday living." Today, corporations call it diversity training. Virgilio had it figured out more than thirty-five years ago.

He didn't stop there. When a French professor by the name of Jacques Audinet came to teach at MACC, he and Virgilio struck up a friendship. Jacques suggested that Virgilio learn French and get his Ph.D. in Paris. At first, Virgilio was startled. "Me? A Mexican American parish priest? Then he thought some more. "Why not me?"

"Your mestisaje teachings are profound. You should write a doctoral thesis on them," Jacques suggested. "Your papers on the subject should be published the world over. Come with me to Paris. I'll help you all I can." And so it happened. A wonderful collaborative friendship blossomed between the two priests that remains strong to this day. Together and individually, they have taken the message of mestisaje to Europe, Latin America, Africa, and Asia as well as to every corner of the United States. In doing so, they have helped improve cultural and human understanding far beyond the west side of San Antonio.

Father Virgil understands the concept of the cosmic habitforce better than anyone I know. He combines faith in his God with faith in himself. He doesn't leave things up to the man upstairs, expecting miracles to fall in his lap. He works it. Relentlessly.

It would be a betrayal to just leave things to God. God wants me to use the intelligence He has endorsed me with to share in the buildup of creation. He has entrusted it to our care. Therefore, I like to live as if everything depended on me, knowing full well that the final outcome depends on God. This gives me a tremendous sense of inner freedom. For whatever the end product is, I know it is for the best.

I believe in God but I don't depend on Him, because he shares his divine intelligence with me. I am not his puppet, rather his partner. None of us are, we were created to be his partner.

And because he believes as he does, miracles fall in his lap most days of the week. That's the cosmic habitforce at work!

Taking the Quantum Leap

When Napoleon Hill first published *Think & Grow Rich* and *The 17 Principles of Personal Achievement,* he had no scientific proof to back up the concept: *"Whatever your mind can conceive and believe, it can achieve."* Even the most respected scientists of the day, Hill's friends Albert Einstein and Thomas Edison, couldn't help him prove it. Still, he convinced millions the world over that our thoughts do in fact become reality.

That was three-quarters of a century ago. Today, a body of scientific proof exists that backs up Hill's work: quantum physics. Often described as the science of possibilities, quantum physics scientifically proves that the mind has the power to create reality. It explains that *whatever reality exists within the brain is more real than whatever exists outside it.* This amazing scientific discovery can be expressed in several ways:

> Whatever is real in your brain eventually becomes real in your life.

Whatever you think about, if repeated often enough, becomes true in real life.

Put to practical use, one can interpret the findings at least two ways:

If you think about success, success becomes real.
If you think about failure, failure becomes real.

You don't have to go to Harvard or Yale to learn about quantum physics. Simply rent the movie *What the #$#! Do We Know?* It gives you a practical, entertaining, and thorough explanation of how science is discovering new and mysterious ways the brain works. In the film, several noted scientists and researchers explain how science can now trace the electrical energy that constitutes our thoughts and connects them to one another. The more often we have the same thought, the more our brain produces receptors that align with this thought, encouraging it to repeat, and allowing it to become more real. The more real it becomes in our mind, the more likely it is to become real in our life.

When I saw the film, I was not surprised. It explained the reality I have known for years. But now, scholars like those who often scoffed at Napoleon Hill's findings are on board. Thinking like we're thinking. It's as though they are giving us the perfect gift-wrapping to this present called *Think & Grow Rich: A Latino Choice.* It proves that the principles outlined in Hill's work and in this book are not theories to be questioned. They are not hypotheses to be proven. They are as real as you. And as real as you make them.

Researchers have proven that intention is a force that creates reality, thus giving us a scientific explanation for why good fortune smiles on the optimist. Because good thoughts inhabit his brain most of the time, they eventually become real! Quantum physics also explains why conscious autosuggestion works. Repeating your goal to yourself six times a day for six months forces your brain to strengthen its neural receptors for that intention. It forces your conscious mind to connect with your subconscious mind to create its own reality. This science also explains why negative thoughts create bad "luck."

There's a song with the line, "If it weren't for bad luck, I'd have no luck at all." What is the attitude of that line? You guessed it. Negative. Next time you get down in the dumps because of something bad that happened, be aware of what you do. If you dwell on your misfortune, your brain will begin to form negative energy. That energy strengthens the brain's receptors with every new negative thought. If you don't consciously catch yourself and change your negative thoughts to positive ones, you will attract more negative energy and more bad luck. Pretty soon, you'll be singing the bad luck song on your way to a big black hole.

The opposite is also true. When you learn to catch yourself in a negative thought after a misfortune, you can turn things around quickly. You can take the experience and turn it into an opportunity. You will learn from your mistake. Only then will your mind be clear enough to think and concentrate on your goal and definite major purpose. Only then will your brain began to build "good luck receptors." Only then will the magic happen. Do this and you'll be back on track before you know it.

When I made up my mind to accept the notion that my mind could achieve anything I could conceive, I didn't hesitate. I didn't look back. I was young and ready to believe. I was ready to change my life. Stuck in a job earning ten cents over minimum wage with a growing family to support, I had to do something. Even though I loved my job and the people I worked with, there was no way I could make a go of things staying where I was and doing what I was doing. *Think & Grow Rich* and *The 17 Principles of Personal*

Achievement changed my life almost immediately. My money worries vanished. I became more confident and eager to believe that anything was possible. My business boomed and I was on my way!

Today, I am financially secure, have built and sold the largest Hispanic ad agency in the United States, advised three presidents, worked with Fortune 500 CEOs, taught at Harvard, received an honorary doctorate from the University of the Incarnate Word, and received enough awards to fill a warehouse (although I don't display them). Looking back, I marvel at my good fortune and thank my God, my wife, my family, my colleagues, and my friends for being a part of my success, and for helping me to enjoy such a splendid life. All because I discovered Napoleon Hill and followed his approach.

My good friend Henry Cisneros, the former HUD secretary under President Clinton, made an insightful observation the other day at breakfast. He said that as Latinos we are lucky to embrace the combined values that make us who we are. As Americans, we value the pursuit of happiness. As Latinos, we simply value happiness. I don't know about you, but I'd say that's a pretty good place to be. For my part, I have enjoyed the pursuit as much as the happiness.

Acknowledgments

When my good friend Adrienne Pulido called to tell me the Napoleon Hill Foundation was looking for someone to write the Latino version of *Think & Grow Rich,* I was ecstatic! She remembered that Napoleon Hill's teachings had changed my life and thought the assignment was made to order for me. She put me in touch with Don Green, the executive director of the Napoleon Hill Foundation, who gave me his blessing and introduced the idea of featuring seventeen successful Latinos to exemplify each of Hill's Principles of Personal Achievement.

I am truly thankful to Adrienne and Don. They gave me the privilege to renew my connection to Napoleon Hill and a grand opportunity to have his teachings impact a new generation. In a sense, my connection with this great man and the impact he had on my life has come full circle.

To the seventeen Latino role models featured in this book: my heartfelt thanks. I enjoyed interviewing sixteen of you and getting to know your story better. In every case, I was inspired and amazed by all you have achieved, all you have contributed to our community, and the beautiful people that you are.

Most of all, I thank my beautiful and gracious wife and partner, Kathy Chapman Sosa, who interviewed Alberto Gonzales. She is the A-team and I gladly follow her lead, especially with regard to everything I write. She reads and improves every line, and this book is no exception.

To my children, grandchildren, and great-grandchildren, to my extended family and friends—especially my brother Robert—my buddy Oscar Vaca and my mentor Lou Agnese: *gracias* for being there through thick and thin.

Lastly, thanks to my mother, born Anna Maria de Jesus Ortiz, and my father, Roberto Jimenez Sosa, who immigrated as children from Mexico to this great country and who, through their courage, gave me my American birthright.

Notes

All quotations from the subject of each chapter are from the author's interviews and are used with permission.

All quotations and paraphrases from Napoleon Hill are from *Napoleon Hill's Keys to Success: The 17 Principles of Personal Achievement,* published by Dutton Books in 1994, and are used with permission of the Napoleon Hill Foundation.

The quote from Samuel P. Huntington in Chapter 1 is from his book *Who Are We?: The Challenges to America's National Identity,* published by Simon & Schuster in 2004.

All quotes from Charles Patrick Garcia in Chapter 2 are from his book *Message From Garcia,* published by John Wiley & Sons, Inc., in 2003, or are from an interview and used with permission.

The quote from Arnold Schwarzenegger in Chapter 2 is from his endorsement to Charles Patrick Garcia's book *Message From Garcia.*

All quotes from President George W. Bush in Chapter 4 are from an interview and used with permission.

The quote from John F. Kennedy in Chapter 4 is from his inaugural address on January 20, 1961.

The quote from Muhammad Ali in Chapter 4 is from his book *The Soul of a Butterfly: Reflections on Life's Journey*, published by Simon & Schuster in 2004.

Peter Drucker is paraphrased in Chapter 12 from *Napoleon Hill's Keys to Success: The 17 Principles of Personal Achievement,* published by Dutton Books in 1994.

Donald Trump is paraphrased in Chapter 12 from *How to Get Rich,* published by The Random House Publishing Group, a division of Random House, Inc., in 2004.

Malcolm Gladwell is paraphrased in Chapter 13 from *Blink: The Power of Thinking Without Thinking,* published by Little, Brown and Company in 2005.

The Reyes Holdings LLC profile in Chapter 17 is from Hoovers Online (www.hoovers.com).

The *Time* magazine profile on Virgilio Elizondo in Chapter 18 is from the article "If Jesus Had Been Born in San Antonio," published in the December 11, 2004, issue.

Index

About the Authors

LIONEL SOSA is an independent marketing consultant, motivational speaker, and portrait artist. He was named one of the twenty-five most influential Hispanics in America by *Time* magazine in 2005. He was a media consultant for President George W. Bush in 2000 and 2004, and has served in that role in six presidential campaigns. Lionel was a Fellow at the Institute of Politics at Harvard University and regularly guest lectures at major universities. He holds an honorary doctoral degree from the University of the Incarnate Word in San Antonio, Texas. He can be reached at LionelSosa.com.

THE NAPOLEON HILL FOUNDATION is a nonprofit educational institution founded by Dr. Hill himself, and based on his famed "Law of Success." It is located on the campus of The University of Virginia's College at Wise.